God's Pageantry:
The Threshold Guardians & the Covenant Defender

God's Pageantry: *The Threshold Guardians & the Covenant Defender*

Published by Armour Books
P. O. Box 492, Corinda QLD 4075, Australia
www.armourbooks.com

Cover Illustration: Cherubim from 'Ezekiel Gallery' by Ted Larson
Interior design and layout by Book Whispers

ISBN: 978-0-980362-07-7

National Library of Australia Cataloguing-in-Publication entry

Creator: Hamilton, Anne, 1954- author.
Title: God's pageantry : the threshold guardians & the covenant defender / Anne Hamilton.

ISBN: 9780980362077 (paperback)

Subjects: Covenant theology.

Devotional literature.

Mythology.

Dewey Number: 231.76

God's Pageantry:
The Threshold Guardians & the Covenant Defender

Anne Hamilton

Armour

This book requires careful reading to be understood and appreciated; a dialogue towards freedom. It delves into the forgotten world of covenants, thresholds and the spiritual forces that operate at doorways, gates of significant opportunity and calling. Anne seeks to address issues either misunderstood or forgotten, as today covenants are made and broken without thought of consequence. Her desire is to help the reader recognise, identify and then counter the effects of dark powers placed at thresholds to impede or abort the believer's access. *God's Pageantry* leaves you with the deep assurance that our God is the God of the breakthrough (Micah 2:13).

Ps. Ben F. Gray
CHI–Ministries
Australian Prayer Network

It is with much joy and honour that I pen this endorsement.
After basking in the pleasant pastures of faith and salvation, this book by Anne Hamilton is as exhilarating as facing high winds on mountain tops and riding through storms at sea while standing hand in hand with God. Anne Hamilton writes with inspiration and revelation from the Holy Spirit, and through her intense journeys and intimate dealings with Father God in her life.
This is a powerful and timely writing released by God.
I am deeply convinced that God has released new wisdom and revelation through Anne for the times that we live in today. He has opened ancient doors so that His people can seek and find the keys to understand their destiny. If you want to unlock the door to your destiny, you need to understand this, and you can only comprehend this book when you are led by the Holy Spirit.
To prepare yourself, I recommend that you have read the first two books in this series:

- *God's Poetry: The Identity and Destiny Encoded in Your Name*
- *God's Panoply: The Armour of God and the Kiss of Heaven.*

You will be magnificently blessed as I have been. There will be an awakening of the deep, deep things inside you. The book will illuminate, like a search light, the deep things of God. You will have the keys to choose hope, and to catch hold of the destiny that God has prepared you for.

However, a warning to all potential readers: This is not a book where you are given a formula and you do things step by step by step. This is not another book on how to decree and proclaim in a novel way. This book is for serious seekers only. If you are not willing to consider throwing away your preconceptions at the foot of the cross, this book is not for you. If you are not willing to open your heart to the Holy Spirit and His leading, you are not ready for this book.

Many people will have waited all their lives for a writing like this, illuminating both the heart of Father God and also the heart of man.

As a serious seeker, you must be committed to seek God and to partner with the Holy Spirit only. The Holy Spirit is the One Who can lead you through the revelation contained in *God's Pageantry* and also to new insights specifically for you. Journey with the Holy Spirit to embrace the love of the Lord Jesus, the Anointed One Who cut the everlasting covenant, Who made it possible and perfect. He is welcoming you into His Kingdom and into His Father's family.

Come away from *God's Pageantry* and dance with the Anointed One!

Donna Ho
Director of the Association of China, Israel and Australia
Friendship, Culture and Economic Exchange (TACIA)

The insight within the pages of this book is simply astounding. For anyone keen to decode their destiny and understand how to step in greater freedom for themselves or for others, we highly recommend this book. We have used the principles here and, as a result, have experienced firsthand breakthroughs that had consistently eluded us before. We have also encountered deeper levels of spiritual authority and found an ease in walking into new seasons through the revelations within the pages of *God's Pageantry*. We feel that, at this moment in history, *God's Pageantry* reveals a lost understanding of threshold covenants—and that this is indeed a crucial key to unlocking doors that will allow us to walk into our destiny. A must read for the days in which we live.

David & Natalie Tensen
Leader Heart Australia
Elijah House Ministries Australia

There are a lot of good books out there, but *God's Pageantry* is an absolute treasure of fresh revelation, insight, and wisdom—a timely, and much needed key for breakthrough for so many of us! Breakthrough for those approaching the threshold of their destiny, breakthrough for those longing to enter into promises and prophetic words received, but never fully realised. Breakthrough for individuals, for the body of Christ, churches, companies, corporations, even nations. I've already read the book through twice; highlighting, underlining, and dog–earing the pages. I recommend it highly as a "must read".

Sandra Sellmer–Kersten
House of Nacham, NZ

I was challenged by *God's Pageantry* to start at the beginning with God's Poetry. They are taking me to a new place of intercession and openness to hearing God. Through them, He is revealing what I need to see and to deal with. Thank you for the blessing of your writing.

Lorna A McDougall DRSAM
Elijah House Ministries Scotland

EPIC — POWERFUL — A FEAST SET BEFORE YOU — ENGAGING — TANGIBLE
Did I mention EPIC? I confess I had never heard about covenant defenders before and entered reading this prayerfully and with a Bible nearby. Therefore this was a massive eye opener! Anne is clearly passionate about the work she undertakes for the Lord and equally clearly is well educated in the topic. I felt safe and confident as a reader. Although I have not yet read two previous books of her work that would help me engage with this particular topic, it can still be read as a standalone work. But I issue caution here. Why? I mentioned a word. FEAST. This is a huge feast of information! On another level entirely. This needs a lot of consuming in small parts. I needed, at times, to sit back and think about what I had just read—and pray.

Louisa Black
Author of *Coming Back Through Grace*

Anne's book is one of the most intriguing and wonderful I have ever read. So many 'Ah ha!' moments. The depth of research is very satisfying and I marvel at the ability of her mind to make connections that only seem obvious in retrospect. This information and line of reasoning has already been useful for me in my work. When I see clients who have had attack after attack of seeming misfortune, I know where to look. And I am finding it just as is described in *God's Pageantry*. I cannot thank Anne enough for her work in putting this book together.

Kerry Horan
Psychologist, Good Counsel International

Very encouraging. Right where I was at, at the time, it lifted me and gave me hope and renewed purpose.

Sharon Flowers

God's Pageantry is genuinely amazing! I found the revelation regarding threshold covenants so interesting and helpful—especially now as we are on the threshold of our destiny. The book gives us the warnings to be very aware of the schemes of the enemy and his ploys, and to be very diligent in our watchman status. In hindsight, I now see that not only the enemy, but we ourselves, have sabotaged our vision. I raise my face for the kiss of Jesus.

Clarice Unwin
Kedesh Ministries, Australia

God's Pageantry is more than a book. It has been a unique and timely God-send. An adventure to read! Filled with 'light bulb' moments that enable you to recognise past threshold challenges and provides key preparation to step into the new. When I reached the last page, I had to turn back to the first, because there was so much to savour and revisit. The layers of insight wrapped in each page are gold, and have been life changing. Not just for me! Anne Hamilton's first-hand experience and close relationship with God reveal layers of insight that are applicable to everyone on a journey to their destiny. There is nothing else in bookstores like it.

Milly Bennitt
Cabin Academy, UK

By the same author

Many–Coloured Realm

The Singing Silence

The Winging Word

The Listening Land

Gawain and the Four Daughters of God:
the testimony of mathematics in Cotton Nero A.x

Coming soon:

Daystar: The Days are Numbered Book 1

IN THIS SERIES

God's Poetry: The Identity & Destiny Encoded in Your Name

Finalist in International Book Awards 2012

Winner of Bronze Medal in eLit Awards 2013

God's Panoply: The Armour of God & the Kiss of Heaven

Winner of Gold Medal in Illumination Awards 2013

Thank You

Dell
Lisa
Alison
Janice
Janette
Janelle
Natalie
Donna
QK
Jon
Ben

Contents

Foreword

'How can Margaret have written *my* story with such uncanny accuracy? She didn't interview *me*!'

Years ago, I was taken aback while reading Margaret Wertheim's book, *Pythagoras' Trousers*, about women studying physics. By the end of the second chapter, the story aligned so closely with my own experience at university, I was stunned. 'Just how common is this?' I wondered.

Just to reassure you at this point: *God's Pageantry* is not a book about physics.

Rather it's about two forgotten covenants of ancient times and their relevance to life today. Yet I have little doubt as we explore threshold covenants, many readers will think: 'How can Anne have written *my* story with such uncanny accuracy? She didn't interview *me*!'

Yes, problematic threshold covenants are *very* common. They're such knotty, thorny puzzles in real life they make theoretical physics look relatively simple. And, despite their complexity, they have—wondrously and amazingly—the very thing all physicists yearn for: an elegant solution.

Name covenants are often precursors to threshold covenants throughout Scripture. This is true both in the Torah and the New Testament where they are repeatedly mentioned as separated by just a few days. Being much simpler than threshold covenants, *God's Pageantry* begins with them.

This book is, like others in this series, by no means the last word on the topic. There are aspects I freely admit I don't understand. So it's meant to open a dialogue on an overlooked problem that has destructive effects on the faith of many people today.

Once again, I am profoundly indebted to friends, family, acquaintances and strangers who have given me permission to use their stories along with their names. It's impossible to discuss identity and destiny while hiding under a pseudonym, so my deepest thanks to you all for your courage, trust and lavish grace.

Prologue

IN THE LAST WEEK OF THE school year, only a dozen students remained in my classroom, all completing work for their final assessment. I was the coordinator of Year 8 mathematics and these last few stragglers were completing a test or some required worksheets.

The mathematics staff at our school gave all students at this year level unlimited chances to pass all tests. We'd inform them right at the beginning of the school year we didn't care about their previous history with the subject. It just wasn't relevant. Our main rule: *You will pass. Everything*.

Passing mathematics is non–negotiable.

We'd tell them the truth: 'No one has ever had to re–do a test more than eight times.'

Eight is a number not so huge that it seems like Everest. It's daunting, but possible.

Kevin was one of the few remaining students who still hadn't fulfilled every requirement for that year. He was sitting near the door, catching the slight breeze that came up across the playing field on sweltering summer days. I went to see how he was going.

His chicken–scratching handwriting covered the paper. But a

quick look told me he'd got full marks so far. On noticing he'd reached the last half page of the last worksheet, I praised him: 'You're almost there. Well done.'

He threw down his pen, jumped up and flung his chair aside. It crashed to the floor and, with an incoherent cry, Kevin ran out the door.

'What caused that?' I asked the aboriginal tutor, open-mouthed.

She set off after him. He was heading across the playing field towards the back gate. Her plaintive voice drifted back to the classroom: 'Kevin, stop! Stop, Kevin! Kevin, I'm old and I'm fat and I'm slow and you're being unfair! How can I possibly catch you?'

Kevin started laughing so much, he actually did stop and allowed himself to be brought back. It took almost half an hour to calm him down and draw out what was distressing him. Finally out of tearful depths I had no idea could be so profound in a thirteen-year-old, he said: 'I've never ever passed anything before. Not even in Year 1. I don't know who I'd be if I did pass.'

Sighing, holding back her own tears, the aboriginal tutor persuaded Kevin that passing was a risk worth taking.

The real tragedy was not that Kevin's identity was bound up in failing, though that is a heartbreaking aspect of it. Rather it's that I took decades to appreciate the depth of his insight. The last page of the last worksheet in Year 8 mathematics is a minor threshold in the cosmic scheme of things. But it's still a threshold.

He was right to wonder who he'd be if he passed it.

Because the threshold into destiny is, always and everywhere, intimately linked to identity. Like Kevin and so many others, I self-sabotaged at thresholds.

Unlike Kevin, I was completely blind to this failing in myself.

1

At the Gate of Heaven

FOR AS LONG AS HUMANITY has existed, people have had legends about what happens after death. One Jewish story has an angel guarding the gates of heaven. His task is to ask a simple question. If the soul wanting admittance can answer it, the gates will be opened wide. But if not, the soul will be turned away. The question?

Just this: '*Who are you?*'

There's no particular trick to this question. However behind it lies a profound thought.

When we were conceived, God breathed into each of us a soul. He did that by naming us. That whisper of love, that God-chosen name, defines both our identity and our destiny.

If we have walked in that calling during life, we will remember our name and be able to answer the angel's question. But if we have turned aside from our calling, we have effectively forgotten who we are. We won't remember our true name when confronted at the gates of heaven and asked for it.

The notion of identity in this century has undergone a radical change.

In the past, many people failed to differentiate between their career and their identity. They saw themselves as 'doctor' or 'farmer', 'mechanic' or 'lawyer'. This was particularly true for people who studied a long time to be able to enter a profession. Somewhere along the way, the effort and dedication of achieving that goal had led to a subtle substitution: vocation for identity.

This kind of mistake still happens.

Another common identity crisis is caused by relationship: when we define ourselves in terms of someone else. 'Wife of,' 'Partner of,' 'Son of'—even 'Manager of' or 'Friend of'—are just a few of the ways we can become known to others. In a family with a celebrity, this imposition of identity can cause friction when it becomes too difficult to emerge from under another person's shadow.

There's also another way relationship can influence identity: some people feel they are nothing without one specific person in their lives. If, for any reason, that person leaves them, the loss is especially intense because they've shaped their identity around the relationship.

And of course there are many superficial expressions of identity: when it becomes all about the looks, the beauty treatments, the car, the house, the designer clothes. Ralph Lauren, the fashion personality, reportedly said: 'The crux of a person's identity ... resides in the trappings, not in the person himself. One needn't be well-read, so long as one surrounds himself with books ... In short ... one can seem to be what one wants to be.'

In Lauren's world, we define ourselves by the luxury holidays, the bank balance or what the kids achieve. As these expressions of identity slide towards obsession, there is also the gun or the game—people so fixated on firearms or video games, they find in them the ultimate expression of self.

In addition, the twenty-first century has produced a hitherto-unrecognised manifestation of identity. There are those who claim a sex act defines their identity.

The fusion of homosexuality with identity is seen by some as a clever and cynical political manoeuvre and by others as a stark and obvious reality. Either way, by defining identity in terms of sexuality, a new player has entered the arena.[1]

Today identity is also often found in a place that didn't exist until this century: connectivity to information. Whether that information is mediated via social media, mobile phone texting or an email account, it is the degree of interaction that counts. Indeed, our digital culture has overturned traditional notions of virtue. YouTube has reshaped an entire generation's view of humility—narcissism is now seen as good and acceptable.

Identity can be about race, tribe, country, religion.

It can even be about memory—some writers suggest total amnesia wipes away identity.[2]

I believe true identity is none of these. It is meant to be a diamond woven with destiny. Far from being a mixed metaphor, that woven stone is, as we shall see, precisely what the angel wants.

Yet when our identity is chained to a career, another person, our bank balance, a video game or a sex act, it's trapped. It's been trivialised and stripped bare. It's been robbed of both purpose and meaning.

How do we discover what we're here on earth for? How do we unveil our true identity? If we look in the mirror and turn the angel's question on ourselves, what answer do we get when we ask, 'Who are *you*?'

Can the riddle of our era—the purpose of life, the meaning of individual identity—really be this simple? Is it just to remember your own name?

Ben held her in his arms while he sat on his Seat of Wisdom ... They gazed at one another in the soft, sawdusty silence. Ben turned his small and precious child under the single yellow light bulb. He gazed at her starfish fingers, seashell ears, pearly nails and rockpool eyes ... On the day of her naming ceremony Saffron was still buttercup fresh, spring lamb new, a little mystery to them all. Ben raised his face to the sky and declared to the universe:

All we know about our fifth daughter is that her hair is more lovely than marigold.

All we know is she is more rare and precious than the costliest spice.

All we know is she is more beautiful to us than Aurora, goddess of the dawn. And for all that we know we name this small and precious mystery 'Saffron Silk'.

Glenda Millard, *The Tender Moments of Saffron Silk*

'Look around the room.'

It was the first session of a mission training–event and the keynote speaker was an eminent psychiatrist. As an 'ice–breaker' he asked us to examine our surroundings. 'Choose a part of the room that attracts you the most. Something that resonates with you personally. Whatever you feel you can identify with. It could be the floor, the ceiling, a window, a chair—anything that arrests your attention.'

I glanced around. The room was quite bare. Nothing 'called' to me in any significant way. I mentally dismissed the game.

But the psychiatrist wasn't finished. 'When you've made your choice, share it with the person next to you.'

He wants us to be serious about this!? I scanned the room again. The front door was quite unusual: its central section was held together by a wooden frame and one spot, near the upper hinge, drew my attention. I turned to the woman sitting next to me, ready to share my choice.

'I know what this is about,' she revealed, 'so it's unfair of me to take part in this exercise. Tell me what you've chosen.'

Gulp. *This is not a random silly game to help us get to know each other? Anyway, can I adequately explain a blank spot? Time to rethink my choice.* 'See that frame around the door?' I asked the woman. 'Not the doorway. The framework that's part of the door. The bit where the hinges are attached so it fixes to the wall.'

She eyed me strangely. 'And what made you choose that?'

'I don't suppose I'd normally have even noticed this door had a special framework around it. But now it's been brought to my attention, I think it's important. It holds that door together.'

The woman's expression changed. She seemed absolutely astonished. I couldn't see that my answer was in any way remarkable but I began to worry as the psychiatrist called our focus back to him. 'Who chose the floor?' he asked. Several hands went up. 'So people walk all over you, do they?'

The shock around the room was palpable.

'Who chose the ceiling?'

A few hands hovered around half-way up.

'So you think you're above the rest of us, do you?'

The hands dropped.

'Who chose the window?' he continued relentlessly.

Hands barely rose now. 'People see right through you?'

'Who chose the door?'

Phew! I was glad I had specifically excluded it.

'People barge right through you?' He looked around the room. 'Anyone decide on anything else?'

The woman next to me said, 'This young lady chose the framework around the door. Because it's important and it holds the door together.'

The psychiatrist turned to me with an expression like that of a hunter who spots a rare, exotic species. *Who are you?* he seemed to ask.

Actually, I am that blank spot right there, on the doorway. Near the hinge.

I didn't dare ask his thoughts about my bizarre, nebulous choice.

Yet, several decades later, I realise it was not *any* blank spot. I hadn't the slightest idea back then of the spiritual significance of that exact position on an entranceway.

That psychiatrist wasn't posing the question he thought he was.

He assumed he was asking about behaviour.

In fact, he was asking about identity.

Today, I'd take him on at his own game. I'd turn on those paralysed people who'd identified with the door and ask: 'So, is your name Janice or Rhoda? Peter or Thomas?'

If they chose the floor, I'd first ask about Tim. For the window, I'd inquire after Val or Gordon. If they'd eyed the ceiling, I'd start with Taylor or Ross. For the chair, it'd be Cath.

To confuse behaviour and identity is a common mistake.

And sometimes even the experts amongst us fall into that trap.

Amongst Christians, there's a tendency to become hooked on a subtle variation of this mistake. We can become so focussed on the gifts of the Spirit that God has endowed us with, we draw our identity from them. It doesn't matter what it is—from administrative skill to prophecy—we're on a dangerous slope if we find our vindication, meaning or identity in the gift, and not in and through Christ.

I don't think life is absurd. I think we are all here for a huge purpose. I think we shrink from the immensity of the purpose we are here for.

Norman Mailer

My dad used to tell a story about my mum and himself. She'd say the problem with their relationship was that he lived on a pedestal. He'd retort the real problem was that she lived in a cellar. She'd counter with: 'Every time I get out of my cellar to connect with you, I can't reach past the base of your pedestal.'

My dad went to the USA for some intensive training in Elijah House prayer ministry and, while there, he found people agreed with my mum.

Taken aback, he gave the problem considerable thought. On his return, he confessed: 'I've realised this pedestal is too high to get down off. But I've got an idea. I'm going to invite Jesus onto it with me. Maybe He'll bring a spiritual ladder.'

My mum decided it was a reasonable plan so, in their quiet time one morning, that's what they prayed. Jesus, according to my dad, almost immediately appeared on the pedestal. He took my dad's hand and jumped.

It was unexpected and alarming.

But then—nothing. No sense of falling, no sense of hitting the ground—in fact, no sense of anything different.

The evening of the following day, some thirty–six hours later, my dad turned to my mum. 'We've landed!' he announced.

'What?' she asked, baffled. 'What are you talking about?'

'Jesus and me. We've just landed.' Dad looked sheepish. 'I didn't know the pedestal was *that* high.'

Identity can get warped by other people's expectations of us, rather than who we really are. My dad's name was James and his mum—just like the mother of James and John, the sons of Zebedee—was very ambitious for him. Zebedee's wife wanted her sons to have precedence in the kingdom she thought Jesus was going to establish—to sit, as she put it, one on His right hand and one on His left.

This was a very careful choice of words on her part. She wanted her sons to fulfil their destiny. And with a name like James, derived from 'jamin', *right hand* or *hand of power*,[3] he was obviously destined to be the right-hand man of someone powerful.

But Jesus had a way of turning the traditional Hebrew understanding about the entwining of destiny within names upside down. He nicknamed James and John 'Boanerges', *sons of thunder*—conforming rather well with the mighty-hand-of-power idea their mum had in mind but certainly ill-fitting for any projected role in the kingdom of grace and peace.

Simon he renamed 'Peter', *the rock*. In the original Aramaic, this was 'Cephas', better translated as *threshold stone* or *cornerstone*—a word which informs so many aspects of the letters Peter wrote about Christ the Cornerstone.

I'd be really interested to know what Jesus thought about Thomas. The man who, for two millennia, has been labelled 'doubting'.

To go down in history for his disbelief when he'd been previously so staunch in his faith is ironical. Clearly the disciples were all aware of the possible trap when Martha and Mary sent word Lazarus was ill. They knew the authorities would use the circumstances as bait and would be lying in wait for Jesus. When He finally announced His intention to head for Bethany, *'Thomas, nicknamed the Twin, said to his fellow disciples, "Let's go, too—and die with Jesus."'* (John 11:16 NLT)

These are words of dauntless courage in the face of supreme danger. Yet, for two thousand years, Thomas has been labelled 'doubting'. His bravery is brushed aside, forgotten. It's as if the defining moment of his identity was encapsulated in that all–too–human incident after Jesus' death when he clung to his conviction that all his friends were stuck in the first stage of grief: denial. After all, who'd ever come back from the dead?

The trouble with such labels is that they can too easily come to define our identity.

Even believers are unbelievably confused about what identity actually is. As I search the internet to discover how people of faith understand 'identity in Christ', I find: *accepted, chosen, justified, redeemed, secure, free, forgiven, established, anointed, sealed, adopted, appointed, reconciled, assured.*

Wonderfully true as these descriptors are, they have nothing to do with identity. They have everything to do with status. Identity is unique and specific to the individual. These descriptors are so generalised, they apply to every Christian. They do not carry any sense of the exclusive, exceptional nature of identity, its passionate individuality and the inimitable, matchless destiny associated with it.

They suggest all names are the same: that it wouldn't matter if I were Anne or Beatrice or Charlotte. The whole of Scripture, however, testifies differently.

What's in a name? That which we call a rose
By any other name would smell as sweet.

William Shakespeare

On the wall of the church I attend each week, there's a picture of a red gash. The rector put it there one Sunday just after Easter to illustrate his sermon. A former architect, he was keen on design, sculpture and modern art. He told the congregation about an exhibition he'd seen in Britain.

One small room was entirely white. At first sight, there appeared to be nothing in it. Then he noticed the touch of the artist, Anish Kapoor: a small red gash high on one pristine wall. *Hmmm,* he mused. *I could've done this. Someone could have paid me megabucks to paint the walls white and draw that pointy red mark that looks like an arrow or a small spear.*

As he moved closer to inspect the red mark, he noticed it wasn't a drawing. A red gash was actually carved into the white wall.

Everything changed when he read the title of the work. The name made all the difference. It transformed a bland, minimalist room with its mundane, almost–empty air into a sacred space.

The name of the work: *The Healing of Saint Thomas.*

The rector felt a tingle of awe as the exquisite symbolism of the room washed across his mind: the red gash represented the spear–thrust in Jesus' side made by a Roman lance; the white walls surrounding him were His spotless sinless body. His mind went back to the story of Thomas' adamant stand against his fellow disciples. Long before psychology discovered the stages of grief, Thomas realised his friends had reverted to denial about Jesus' death. 'I won't believe,' he said, 'unless I can touch the wounds made by the nails and put my hand in His side.'

The rector took a deep breath. A curious sense of peace pervaded the room. *I'm inside the Body, I'm within the purity and healing.*

He realised how wrong he'd been. He decided he could never have even conceived of something so simple that engendered so much reverence.

In real life, unlike in Shakespeare, the sweetness of the rose depends upon the name it bears. Things are not only what they are. They are, in very important respects, what they seem to be.

Hubert H. Humphrey

A name makes all the difference.

It converts a void into a sacred space.

It confers meaning.

It lays down story and history—instantly.

And if all this is true for a small white room in an art exhibition, how much more so for people!

Naming gives soul.

Back in the first chapters of Genesis, *the book of beginnings,*[4] we have the description of humanity's creation.

And the Lord God formed man of the dust of the ground,[5] *and breathed [*neshima*] into his nostrils the breath [*nashamah*] of life; and man became a living soul [*neshama*].*

Genesis 2:7 HNV

The significance of these very first words for *breath* and *soul* did not elude the Jewish rabbis of old. Christians are often familiar with the Hebrew word 'ruach' for *spirit, wind* and *breath* since it is used to identify the Holy Spirit. Rarely, however, do we know the word for *breathing*, neshima, or its relation, neshama, for *soul.*

As a consequence we miss what the rabbis noticed: the words for *breathing* and *soul* contain the word for *name*, shem.[6]

In their understanding, God imparts life, breath and soul simply by giving us a name.

Just as the artist, Anish Kapoor, changed a white room into a hallowed space through naming, so, long ago, God converted the dust of the earth into a glorious human body through naming.

'Adam,' He breathed.

The first Adam was word made flesh. So are we. God breaths life into a soul, so the rabbis said, not simply through naming us but by giving us part of His own name.[7] When the Father whispers to our unformed frame, He confers identity and destiny as He offers life itself.

The second Adam is Word made flesh. Like Saint Thomas, we need healing. Because the identity and destiny God offered us when He named us needs to be redeemed. And that is only possible through the body and blood of Jesus.

It doesn't matter how many Spirit-filled meetings you've been to throughout your life or how many personal prophecies you've been given—none or thousands. No prophecy compares to that spoken over you by the Lord Himself before you were born: your true name.

And surprising as it may seem, I believe most parents get it mostly right.[8]

'I have called you by name; you are Mine ...'

Isaiah 43:1 NLT

For thousands of years names were considered a source of ultimate power. The 'true name' of an individual was considered to embody the essence of the person and to offer anyone who knew it power over that person.

Knowing the name of a god or goddess meant power over that deity. The Romans were notorious for seeking the secret names of the guardians protecting territories with which they were at war. Using the technique *elicio*, they would invite those gods to Rome.

The historian Livy describes Camillus, ruler of Rome in 396 BC, breaking the siege of the Etruscan city of Veii with this prayer and *elicio*:

'Guided and inspired by your will, Pythian Apollo, I go forth to destroy the city of Veii. To you I devote a tenth part of the spoils. And to you, Queen Juno, now dwelling in Veii, I beseech you to follow us after our victory to our city, which will become your city. There we will build you a temple worthy of your sublime majesty.'

At the time of Alexander the Great, the people of Tyre became concerned for their colossal statue of Apollo. What if Alexander were to entice it away, preparatory to an attack? They fastened it with gold chains.

Images of Ares—the Greek equivalent of the Roman war god, Mars—were secured with magical bindings in several places of Asia Minor to ensure his protection did not suddenly disappear.[9]

Names are power. The whole of the ancient world knew it.

Today it's rare to find the concept outside of a fantasy novel.[10]

Although Jesus is the 'Name above all names', many Christians are not really sure what that means. The apostles used it to great effect, healing the sick, raising the dead, casting out demons.

They were so impressive that people like Simon Magus wanted to emulate them. In fact, an exorcism by the seven sons of Sceva went badly wrong as a result of such ambition:

Some Jews who went around driving out evil spirits tried to invoke the name of the Lord Jesus over those who were demon-possessed. They would say, 'In the name of the Jesus whom Paul preaches, I command you to come out.' ... One day the evil spirit answered them, 'Jesus I know, and Paul I know about, but who are you?' Then the man who had the evil spirit jumped on them and overpowered them all ... they ran out of the house naked and bleeding.

Acts 19:13–16 NIV

The difference is, of course, that Paul had faith and the sons of Sceva didn't.

But 'faith' is both the most profound, as well as the most superficial, difference in this situation. Some Christians tend to wave 'faith' around as a vague catch-all answer. It's a convenient—but ultimately altogether shallow way—to explain why God responds to some prayers and not others. Anyone with simplistic views about it should be compelled to read the book of Job every day for a month.

Yet we can't use the inexplicability of God's purposes as an excuse, either.

The sons of Sceva had faith in the name of Jesus. They wouldn't have done what they did otherwise. Moreover, they were very specific about *which* Jesus. It was a popular name at the time, so they made sure there was no ambiguity about the person behind the name.

So while they had faith in the name of Jesus, they didn't have faith *in* Jesus Himself.

The dimension of relationship was missing. As a consequence, they didn't have access to the faith *of* Jesus.

The apostles used far more than their own faith by invoking the name of Jesus. Because of their name covenant with Him, they had access to His faith, His prayers, His intercession with the Father.

The story of the woman who secretly touched the hem of His garment indicates this joining of faith to Jesus' prayers. The Greek text says she fingered his *kraspedon*,[11] the tassels on his prayer shawl, and was instantly healed of a blood loss condition of twelve years' duration.

No wonder Jesus knew she was there. She didn't simply grab hold of a woollen tuft, she latched on to His prayer life, His relationship with the Father.

God
I barely know you
yet you know me bare
every hair
numbered
each tear

bottled
every thought
known
even before it entered
my mind ...

but

how can I know you?
how capture your thoughts
read your mind
sense your spirit
whisper your words
unless
I step over the threshold
of the door
you hold open
for me?

Janette Fernando, *Knowing God*

Although Thomas is invariably listed as Aramaic for *twin*,[12] I feel Anish Kapoor's profound re–visitation highlights a deeper sense.

The Hebrew word ta'am, *double*, is apparently the root. Tamar is the mother of the second set of twins recorded in the Bible: Perez and Zerah. She was the daughter–in–law of Judah, who fathered her children.

Tamar means *palm tree* and while, on the surface, it seems irrelevant to Tom, *twin*, we should constantly bear in mind God cares far more for prophecy and poetry than any etymological niceties. Perhaps there is a prophetic relationship in the names.

I believe that, rather than simply meaning *twin*, Thomas is also related to either the Greek name, Ptolemy, or to the Hebrew, Bartholomew. Ptolemy means *aggressive, war–like, exceedingly violent* while Bartholomew is *son of Talmai*, that is, *son of many furrows.* Talmai is often translated as *ploughman* or *farmer.*[13]

Ptolemy and Talmai have a common root. In Greek mystery religion, the god Triptolemus had agricultural overtones. In rites enacting his mythic story, he was found in a furrow. The meaning of his name, *triple-ploughing or triple warrior*, suggests both Talmai and Ptolemy. Although we traditionally consider farming as peaceful, a ploughman gashes the earth. These names therefore share overtones of *exceedingly violent.*

Ptolemy is a name made famous by one of Alexander the Great's generals. He took Egypt in the division of territory after Alexander's death at the gateway to India.

Talmai is a name more ancient still. In Scripture it first appears in reference to one of the sons of Anak.

This giant descendant of the Nephilim lived at Hebron. The twelve spies scouting the Promised Land encountered him and were awed by his gargantuan size. They felt as small as grasshoppers. Only Caleb and Joshua weren't intimidated by him.

The report of the spies so worried the Israelites that they were consumed with doubt about going forward. On the very threshold of the Promised Land, they yielded to their fears and turned back.

Forty-five years later, Caleb returned to Hebron and expelled Talmai, Ahiman and Sheshai, the sons of Anak.

It's more than possible Talmai and Ahiman were twins, since Ahiman can mean *my brother is like me.*

While I was investigating the name Thomas, I met a woman who asked me what it meant. She hoped to get enough insight to forge a better relationship with her son. I told her I believed its overall original sense was not so much *the one who has doubts* but *the one who causes doubt.*

She laughed uproariously and said that summed her son up perfectly. 'Tom doesn't have any doubts,' she said. 'He is so self-confident he causes everyone else to have them! In fact, he intimidates me with his assertiveness.'

So if Thomas ultimately derives from Talmai, *the one who causes doubt,* then the reason the apostle John chose to include the episode of Jesus confronting Thomas in his gospel is evident. It's not just about faith or doubt, it's about redeeming the past.

Talmai, a likely twin and a son of Anak, caused doubt.

Thomas, a twin and a disciple of Christ, had doubts.

The defining moment a millennium and a half previously in the history of Israel was abruptly reversed. The twelve tribes of Israel had been on the threshold of a new beginning: they were ready to take possession of Canaan. Twelve men represented the tribes. Two of them stood firm in believing that the promises of God would be fulfilled if they went ahead. Ten doubted.

In the upper room a week after the Resurrection, this situation was reversed. Again there are twelve men, representing the twelve tribes. But this time, ten of them stood firm in their belief the promises of God had been prophetically fulfilled and that Jesus had been raised from the dead. The other two men formed an opposing front. Judas was dead—having committed suicide—the supreme expression of doubt. Thomas expressed his scepticism: he wanted to touch the gash in Jesus' side.

The two situations are mirror images. In both instances, twelve men represent the twelve tribes of Israel. In both instances, they were on the threshold of a new beginning. In one instance, faith was overwhelmed by doubt; in the other, doubt was overwhelmed by faith.[14]

Thomas, post-Pentecost, went on to become one of the men who turned the world upside-down. Ptolemy, Alexander's general, came to the threshold of India but could not take it. Thomas did what Ptolemy couldn't. Two millennia after he told the people of the sub-continent the Good News, the Nasrani of Kerala in India trace their churches back to his evangelistic work.

I have spent my days stringing and unstringing my instrument while the song I came to sing remains unsung.

Rabindranath Tagore

Ptolemy may not have subjugated India but, as one of Alexander's highest-ranking generals, he received a portion of the conquered territory in the division of the spoils. His share included the land of Israel. Thereafter, the Hebrew language was supplanted by the tongue of the victors: Greek.

This intertestamental time was a period of extreme constriction for the Jewish people, as the terrible history recorded in the books of the Maccabees demonstrates. The era began with Ptolemy I Soter, the king who was once a Macedonian general. His name shares common associations with Talmai—first recorded as the name of one of the Anakim, the descendants of Anak.

Anak is said to mean *long-necked* or *necklace*. However its root is *to choke, throttle* or *strangle*.

Talmai and his brothers worried almost all the spies sent out on a reconnaissance mission when the Israelites were on the verge of reaching the Promised Land: perhaps it's no coincidence that 'worry' comes from a German word meaning *strangle*. The sons of Anak effectively acted as threshold guardians.

As constrictors, they mirror today's spiritual guardians who attempt to worry us sufficiently to choke the life out of us as we approach the threshold of destiny.

Jentezen Franklin in *The Spirit of Python: Exposing Satan's Plan to Squeeze the Life Out of You* rightly identifies Python here, showing the various tricks used to deceive us.

However, Python is not the only demonic entity on the threshold.

The three sons of Anak parallel, in my view, a triad of watchers specifically appointed by the forces of hell to prevent each of us coming into our destiny. Moreover, they have legal ground to be there if we have not renounced any ungodly covenants our ancestors took out. Jentezen Franklin does not mention these two other spirits.

Python harassed Paul and Silas during their evangelistic work at Philippi. A slave girl with a Python spirit followed them, calling out and advertising their mission. Paul turned on the girl, cast out the spirit of divination—and then their troubles began. The girl had been a lucrative earner for her masters, who dragged Paul and Silas off to the magistrates.

Python is the same spirit Camillus invoked as he used *elicio* to entice the goddess Juno away from her Etruscan homeland to become a leading figure in the Roman pantheon. The Python spirit was renowned in the ancient world as peculiarly attached to the temple at Delphi which was across the bay from the port of Corinth. There a sibyl called the Pythoness would offer riddles foretelling the future to those who came seeking guidance from her. She sat, babbling her prophetic words in a delirious language, on a bronze tripod above a crevice from which intoxicating fumes emanated. Paul's first letter to the Corinthians, particularly the famous chapter 13, clearly alludes to how to deal with Python, without ever naming it. Not surprisingly, if every choice is based on love, Python is powerless.

Jentezen Franklin relates several encounters with Python. Much is typical in his accounts but extremely atypical aspects are evident too. Franklin overcame Python with relative ease compared to anyone I've ever known in similar circumstances. He mentions wasting but doesn't regard this as the activity of a separate spirit. Nor does he note the possibility others can throw you to Python as a sacrifice in order to achieve their own destiny. Nor does he mention covenants that govern thresholds.

It's likely that, because his family background consists of an evangelist father and faithfully praying mother, these issues were never in contention. The ungodly covenants which give Python so much legal power were, I suspect, dissolved in his parents' generation, if not previously.

Despite the lack of discussion about covenants, inappropriate sacrifices and Python's allies, I highly recommend the book. Nevertheless, there is much left unsaid.[15] For those of us who are Christians but have never dealt with any of the covenants passed down from previous generations, it may not be as comparatively simple to deal with Python as Franklin suggests. Not that he actually suggests that it is particularly simple.

Yet, without an understanding of the four major covenants and how they can go disastrously wrong, we are more likely to be complicit with Python's agenda than refuse to accept its lies. Without an intimate knowledge of the nature of the divine armour God has specifically designed to help us cross over the threshold, we're likely to forget to use it.

Yes, the threshold guardians attack our memory.

It's a vastly efficient way to confuse both our identity and destiny: to simply make us forget. So we can't answer the angel's question.

Jesus told him, 'Anyone who puts a hand to the plough and then looks back is not fit for the Kingdom of God.'

Luke 9:62 NLT

It may seem surprising to find Jesus directly addressing the question of spiritual giants. It's all too easy to miss His allusion to one of the sons of Anak here, the ploughman Talmai. If you look back while ploughing, the furrows will become crooked, not straight.

Jesus was responding to a man willing to follow him and join the band of itinerant disciples, but requesting permission to do just one thing first. The nature of life is such that, when we reach the threshold into our destiny, there will always be something we feel we need to finish first.

Python doesn't often need to dangle any temptation. We all too frequently put ourselves into its clutches through duty or a desire to complete something good that is actually irrelevant to our true calling.

We therefore become complicit with the Constrictor. As Jesus so bluntly points out, we aren't fit for the Kingdom of God. Just as the Israelites weren't fit for the Promised Land when they ignored Caleb and Joshua and listened instead to the spies who had been intimidated by Talmai and his brothers.

However, just because we're unfit at one time doesn't mean God will not give us a second chance.

We may have muffed the first furrow by looking back but God can redeem the situation. It will, however, be in His time, not ours.

That first furrow is the most important. If it's straight, then it's simple enough to keep the rest in line by having one of the oxen walk down the first furrow. If the first furrow is crooked, the rest will likely become even worse. Soon the field may be a disaster zone and all the initial work wasted because the farmer has tried to steer by looking over his shoulder.

Art Kohl says: 'Too many of us try to steer our lives by looking back. We look back and blame our crookedness on our bad home life, environment, circumstances, abuse, parents, teachers, church, or society ...'[16]

The trouble with looking back is we bring those beliefs of the past with us, instead of leaving them behind. And those beliefs form the cords Python uses to bind us as it tries to choke our destiny to death and deliver us into the hands of the Waster.

The fighting strength of a python is in the driving blow of his head backed by all the strength and weight of his body. If you can imagine a lance, or a battering ram, or a hammer weighing nearly half a ton driven by a cool, quiet mind living in the handle of it, you can roughly imagine what Kaa was like when he fought.

Rudyard Kipling, *The Jungle Book*

Elie Wiesel, a Jewish writer who survived the Holocaust, won the Nobel Peace Prize in 1986. His numerous books include a study of the Hasidic masters of the Jewish faith, *Souls on Fire*. In it, he makes a point very similar to the story, which opens this chapter, about the angel guarding the gates of heaven and checking if we remember who we are.

He is often quoted as saying that, when we stand before our Maker to give a reckoning of how we used our lives and talents, we're not going to be quizzed on why we didn't become a messiah or find a cancer cure. We're going to be asked who we are, not what we did.

'Why didn't you become "you"?' is the question we'll have to answer.

This quote attributed to him isn't accurate. Only the idea is. It stems from his story of two brothers: severe, demanding Elimelekh and innocent, suffering Zusia.[17]

Zusia, always happy, always laughing, said, 'When I face the celestial tribunal, I shall not be asked why I was not Abraham, Jacob or Moses. I shall be asked why I was not Zusia.'

'Why aren't you "you"?'

Tough question. Tougher still are: *why did you give in to the constriction and the wasting? Why did you agree with the enemy of your soul?*

For myself, I can't think of reasons, just excuses. As I struggle to know who 'Anne' is created to be and wrestle with aligning the desires of my heart to that design, I am increasingly conscious that, for many of us, the threshold is a perilous place.

I often use the daunting phrase 'constriction and wasting' in reference to a threshold. It's not my own; I've borrowed it from Ben Gray. Yet people are almost always shocked by this phrase. Three words have summed up the entirety of what's happening in their lives. So many people identify with the phrase they think I have an uncanny insight into their personal situation. When I ask if a disaster happened on the very day they thought the door was opening wide into their calling, they are incredulous I know the exact timing.[18]

The truth is that I don't have any special insight. I just know how a threshold operates.

The calling God has empowered us to achieve through what we are called—our true name—is our destiny. Our names tell us not just who we're supposed to be but what we're supposed to achieve in God's kingdom.

Despite this, in today's technology-adoring world, identity is morphing yet again into another bizarre form. Some people's worth used to be measured by who their friends were, so they could name-drop. Now, however, worth is defined by the number of followers we have on various forms of social media.

Imagine that angel at the gate of heaven, completely disinterested in the cure for cancer I've discovered and turning me away because I don't have enough Facebook followers. Somehow I can't see it.

As for that cure for cancer, I doubt if I'm called to discover it—indeed, I don't believe I have the name for it.

Does anyone? Perhaps. On reading years ago about the work of a father and son, both named Ernest Krebs, I thought they had to be the best possible candidates for the ultimate breakthrough in this area. If anyone is destined to find the answer, I'd rate someone named 'Krebs'—German for *crab* or *the constellation Cancer*—top of my list.

Does this sound facetious? Even ridiculous?

While our culture has trained us to think it's absurd to even consider the possibility, Scripture is replete with examples of lives spelled out in the meanings of people's names, as well as in puns and poetry.

Abram, Isaac, Jacob, Eve, Samuel, Achan, Bathsheba, Saul ... to name just a few I've looked at previously in *God's Poetry*.

Revisiting Goliath, we can note one of its meanings is *the one who exiles*. We can also note the Hebrew name David rhymes with the word for *exiled* or *wanderer*. Their conflict, followed by Saul's obsessive jealousy which forces David to flee into exile, seems almost like a fated event.

Yet all names offer us a choice. We are not fated, we are called into the destiny which God prepared for each of us before the foundation of the world. We don't have to answer His summons. Few of us do.

Yet Ephesians 2:10 NKJV tells us: *For we are His workmanship, created in Christ Jesus for good works, which God prepared beforehand that we should walk in them.* It's not particularly obvious in the English translation but the word 'workmanship' (sometimes rendered as 'masterpiece') actually comes from the Greek word for a *poem*.

We are God's poetry: that's what the verse says.

Surprisingly, science concurs! At least to a degree: biological engineers use 'poesis', *human construction*, to describe DNA manipulation.[19] Yet it's from 'poesis' we derive *poem*.

In Scripture we find dozens of examples concerning the destiny of people and places which have more to do with poetry than the original meaning of their names.

Despite substantially agreeing with my thesis in *God's Poetry*, my mum always harboured significant doubts as to whether names really do carry an individual's destiny. 'Is it possible,' she'd sometimes ask, 'that the people and places in Scripture were named *after* the event, not *before*?'

In some cases, I conceded she might well have a point.

But, in the majority, clearly not. There were too many prophecies, especially about places, keyed to already existing names.

Other people had different doubts. They were not so sure about name covenants. The concept was unfamiliar—utterly strange.

I soon realised from the feedback that the reason many of us don't understand name covenants is simple: we don't understand covenants. We tend to think of them as contracts with a special solemnity—perhaps with sacred overtones. Most of us don't realise the purpose of a covenant is oneness.[20] That's what differentiates it from a contract.

The covenant God cut with Abraham extends to the Jewish people even today and on indefinitely into the future. Covenants are forever. That's another essential aspect to them.

Good covenants go on endlessly, so do bad covenants. The staggering implications of this are almost always overlooked.

Eventually my mum was persuaded about name covenants. It wasn't so much Scripture that changed her mind—though naturally that was part of it—as a compelling example in the life of someone she thought she knew well. Before we turn to that case, let's look again at a great forerunner of faith and how his name played into his destiny: Abraham.

But the Hebrew word, the word timshel—'Thou mayest'—that gives a choice. It might be the most important word in the world. That says the way is open. That throws it right back on a man. For if 'Thou mayest'—it is also true that 'Thou mayest not.'

John Steinbeck, *East of Eden*

Abram was a wandering herdsman when God singled him out and chose him to be His friend. Along with his father, Terah, he left Ur of the Chaldees and set out towards Canaan. When they reached Haran, they turned aside from the journey for a while and … delayed … and delayed … This is not particularly surprising, really, since Terah means *turn away* or *delay*. No doubt he was named for his slow birth but here the name epitomises the only thing we really know about him: that on the journey to Canaan, he stopped for so long Abram eventually set out once again without him.[21]

The people of Israel look back to Abram as their ancestor: the daring man of faith who had an intimate acquaintance with God—indeed, the only man in all of Scripture designated 'Friend of God'.

God gave him several promises about his destiny. He said, 'I will bless you and you will be a blessing.'

Now the English language hides what's going on in this statement. God was preparing the ground, working on the most powerful aspect of Abram's identity. Long before the name exchange which converted Abram to Abraham, God was shaping his name.

'I will bless you' is *abrak.* In Hebrew poetry, 'head rhyme' is as important as 'tail rhyme' is in English and here we have a wonderful example: *abrak* and *Abram*.

In the first book in this series I discussed the immense influence of poetry on the destiny encoded in a name. Many people do in fact recognise the significance of what they are called in relation to their calling. However they attribute the impact of their name solely to its meaning, nothing else.

Here's one of the first of many Scriptural examples showing God the poet at work: Abram's destiny was to be a blessing to all humanity. This begins with a rhyme on his name: *abrak*.

Abrak does not have the same meaning as Abram, *exalted father*. Nor does it have the same meaning as the name he later receives as a result of a covenantal exchange of names: Abraham.

God had shown Abram the inky expanse of the night sky in a vision. He'd taken him out and displayed the wonders of its galactic clusters and whorls of shimmering lights. And as the most-distant stars sang the first song of a youthful creation,[22] God told him that his descendants would be as uncountable and numerous as those heavenly lights.

However, Abram obviously had problems with delay. Maybe it had something to do with his relationship with his own father and that stopover in Haran. As the fulfilment of his hope is deferred longer and longer, his wife Sarai comes up with a sure-fire plan to help God out.

Abram should have known better. He'd already believed God and had his faith counted as righteousness. However, eleven years after he left Haran, he fell in with Sarai's scheme and had a son by her maid, Hagar.

Another thirteen years go by.

God appears—unexpectedly. And He has a truly remarkable announcement. His revelation is not about Abram this time. It's about Himself.

'I am El Shaddai,' He says. 'The Lord Almighty.'

2

Fattened for the Kill

HAIMONA WAS SEA-MAD. He only ever wanted to be a naval captain. He'd made meticulous plans from childhood, joining cadets at one school and sea scouts at another. He'd ensured his mathematics courses in his senior years included navigation and he'd put in his application for officer training college the day he was eligible.

To his joy he was accepted. He had no illusions: he knew a long hard road lay ahead of him but he flung himself into his studies with enthusiasm. This was what he'd always wanted.

Before the first day was out, he had trouble hearing his lecturers speak. A day later, his increasing difficulty in listening morphed into hearing voices that weren't there.

Before the first week was out, he was in hospital and was quickly transferred to the wing for mental patients. Haimona was diagnosed with schizophrenia and any possibility he had of pursuing a naval career was in tatters.

He could barely comprehend what had happened. He asked the question all of us throw up at heaven sooner or later: *Why, God?*

He was baffled that the very career he'd always felt called to was now permanently barred to him. That all his work and planning was a waste. Years of relentless, inexplicable struggle to forge a new identity for himself followed.

Yet if we focus on two significant issues here—threshold and name—we may be able to make explicable what seems inexplicable. There are of course physical, psychological and spiritual components in any such complex incident. Some would be so deeply hidden they may never be uncovered. They don't necessarily have to be: the spiritual components of the situation are relatively easy to bring to the light and they hold out a key towards understanding this life–shattering event.

The moment we head towards our true calling in life, we approach a spiritual threshold. Python and its colleagues are alerted and spring into action. The moment we actually step onto that threshold, a spiritual dynamic comes into play.

Just this week, as I handed over my keys to the mechanic servicing my car, he got a call from a woman, frantic because her car had broken down and it was the first day of her new job. The week before, a new worker at my place of employment didn't turn up for the first three days: he'd been so sick he couldn't walk.

These events are more frustrating than life–shattering but they nevertheless hint of the real nature of spiritual thresholds.

The beckoning doorways, the unexpected openings, the fresh beginnings, the new stages: these are liminal places. We treat them casually but Scripture never does. It has a special name for a threshold: a cornerstone.

Now, not every door in life swings open into destiny—into the true calling God has established for each of us to walk in—but those places that do are heavily fortified with specifically–tailored armaments.

We're talking bespoke weaponry here: it is purpose–designed especially for its target. It's not wide–spray; it does not take down everyone in sight. There is nothing random about it. It is a missile built with a particular individual in mind.

Yes, the bullets really do have your name written on them.

Names are not just prophetic encodings of identity. They are also carriers of destiny.

The attack on Haimona was specifically directed at his name. It was designed to smash both his destiny and identity at the most opportune moment to ensure it would never recover.

Haimona is not a threshold name in and of itself. However, as the

Māori form of Simon, it has been associated for over two millennia with the most significant of all threshold names: Cephas, the Hebrew cognate of Peter.

Simon the fisherman was given the name Cephas because he was the first to confess Jesus as the Messiah. Cephas doesn't simply mean *rock*—it comes from the word for a cornerstone, the hollow basinstone placed at a threshold to catch the blood of sacrifice. When the blood of a lamb or goat was painted around the door, it would drip onto this cornerstone.

So for two thousand years, the name Simon has been intimately linked with a threshold word. All thresholds are places of power and imminent danger, but more so if your name happens to be in any way associated with a threshold.

Now the psychological aspects of schizophrenia are very tangled but the spiritual aspects are generally quite simple. In the realm of the spiritual, schizophrenia is powered by two vows. One of these vows is hidden and may have to do with almost anything. However, the other is always along these lines: 'I refuse to hear this. You will never make me listen to this.'

It doesn't just manifest itself with these vows full–blown. They've been there a while waiting for the right trigger. When that trigger happens along, suddenly there's a physical problem merging with a psychological and a spiritual one: it's not about voices but ultimately about willingness to listen.

And what does the name Simon mean?

It comes from Simeon: *to hear with acceptance, to hear and obey, to listen, to hearken.*

The spiritual aspect of Haimona's problem was all about his name. And when did it first manifest?

On the day he stepped into his destiny.

Of course.

For many men that stumble at the threshold are well foretold that danger lurks within.

William Shakespeare, *Henry VI*

Sometimes it's not on the first rung of the ladder when the enemy strikes. Sometimes it's right at the top. Gordon Dalbey speaks of Satan fattening men for the kill. In *Fight like a Man: Redeeming Manhood for Kingdom Warfare*, he tells Steve's story.

I'd like to think such stories are unusual but, tragically, they are not. They're not restricted to men, either.

Steve was married with two adult children. Twenty–five years previously, in pre–marital counselling, his wife had revealed she'd been molested as a child. However, the pastor had told them not to worry because all that had been taken care of on the Cross. Things of the past, he said, cannot harm Christians.

A few decades on, Steve's hard work had been rewarded with an influential position at work. He was about to be appointed senior elder in his high–profile church of several thousand members. But, after the children left home, his wife abruptly announced she hated men and was filing for divorce. She refused counselling.

Shocked, the church officials barred Steve from all levels of leadership. Not only was his marriage destroyed but his witness at work and in the community too.

In this all–too–common story, one sentence leapt out at me: 'when Steve had finally reached the *threshold* of community esteem and significant ministry, the Enemy struck.'

Thresholds aren't always at the beginning. Sometimes the most crucial are positioned at the final doorway into significant ministry.

Many of us are fattened, exactly as Dalbey says, for the kill.

Luchelle had vast talent as a playwright and missions director.

She'd prepared an innovative programme to present on beaches to holiday-makers during summer. The centrepiece was an allegorical pantomime of a Ringmaster and Son who together create a marvellous world for their clowns. The Jester appears and hoodwinks the clowns into playing with some forbidden toys.

This concept showcased the gospel and God's plan of salvation in an entertaining and metaphorical form. It took years to plan and bring to fruition. There were bright, colourful costumes to make, cleverly-designed sets to build, music to prepare, roles to rehearse, gymnastics to practise ... prayer to undertake.

And the day before she set off on the road—everything ready at last—her world began to fall apart. Her husband—whose role in the pantomime was the ringmaster—abruptly made it clear he had never cleaved to her as his wife. The family he grew up in was his priority emotionally and financially. Broken, she agreed to his ruling, allowing herself to be sacrificed in order for the show to go on the road the following day.

For the spirits of the threshold, timing is everything.

The threshold is the place of expectation.

Johann Wolfgang von Goethe

Jan had taken some marginalised people and worked with them for months, perfecting a theatre production which incorporated a gospel presentation. With her husband's help, she'd taken the show on a regional tour. Much acclaim followed. The finale had been an evening's performance in their own church with over a thousand people attending.

The buzz was electrifying. They were elated to see the growth in the people they were mentoring and also have an opportunity to show their home church just how they'd managed to take the gospel 'on the road'.

The next morning they were asked to see the church's senior pastor. Jan was on a high after the previous evening and thought he was going to discuss a commissioning service. She believed it was his intention to bless their work with the marginalised, and talk about how it could be expanded.

Instead the pastor asked them to give up the theatre troupe entirely as well as all the work with those on the fringes. He wanted them to devote their time to overseeing the church's Sunday School.

Obediently, they sacrificed what they thought was their true calling. Their destiny, in fact.

Just as they believed they'd finally come into it.

When I first heard Jan's story, I wondered if she could have refused to do what the pastor asked. In her view an irreconcilable rift would have resulted and, sooner rather than later, she and her husband would have had to leave the church.

Python certainly knows how to put on the squeeze. It's had millennia of practice.

People named Jan are particularly vulnerable at thresholds. Although naming books almost invariably cite Jan as a derivative of John, I point out in *God's Poetry* it probably comes from Janus, the two-faced Roman god of the doorway. The name covenant locked into Jan is fused with a threshold covenant. This is not the case with every name, still it's far from rare.

Jan and her husband didn't stay long in the clutches of Python.

Their choice to sacrifice their destiny put them instead into the hands of the spirit of Rachab. Aptly known as 'the do-nothing', Rachab is a spirit of wasting.

The stories of those who find themselves in Rachab's clutches are heart-breaking. These are those 'fattened for the kill'.

The classic biblical example is Rehoboam, son of Solomon.

Rehoboam's name means *enlarge the nation* but it also contains the Hebrew for Rachab.

The word rachab is identical to the name Rahab. However, to avoid confusion, I'm using a legitimate alternative spelling to differentiate between Rahab of Jericho and Rachab, spirit of wasting. Both rahab and rachab mean *to spread out, to enlarge, to broaden, to be arrogant.*

Rehoboam was given an ambitious name. Obviously it was intended as a political prophecy about David's line: Rehoboam would enlarge the territory ruled by his father Solomon and become an even greater king.

Ironically, exactly the opposite happened.

When Rehoboam came to the throne, his contempt for his older advisors led to a permanent split in his father's legacy: the kingdom divided into Judah and Israel. There's no real surprise there: *arrogance* is part of his name. The fact he did not *enlarge the nation*, as his name prophesied, reminds us that, while names announce our destiny, our choices determine whether or not we achieve it.

We are called. Not fated.

Rahab the inn-keeper of Jericho is probably Rahab, the wife of Salmon and mother of Boaz. She would therefore be the mother-in-law of Ruth and the great-great-grandmother of David.

Regardless of her place in the genealogies of Israel, as the inn-keeper at Jericho she was—like the spirit which shares her name—a threshold guardian.

A cornerstone covenant obviously existed between her and the two spies she lodged. It's possible she didn't have a clue what their mission was until far too late. However, the very act of offering them hospitality meant that, the moment they passed over the threshold, a cornerstone covenant came into play.[23]

She *had* to defend them to the death. Or suffer the consequences.

They *had* to reciprocate. Or suffer the consequences.

Moreover, under the covenant, they *had* to protect her family. Or suffer the consequences.

Hence why she lied for them. Hence too why they were so concerned about their responsibility for her family and insisted on the scarlet rope. They wanted the understanding to include a condition that any curses for breaking covenant would not fall on them, if her family were harmed accidentally.

The scarlet rope is often seen as a 'type', illustrating the covering of the blood of Jesus—however, it is more immediately a 'type' of the blood of the sacrifice which solemnised a cornerstone covenant.

By undertaking a covenant with the spies, Rahab and her family became part of the children of Israel.[24] Today we'd think of her as racially a Canaanite, but the Israelites would not have. The covenant obliterated that distinction.

In his gospel, Matthew mentions only four women in his genealogy of Jesus. Rahab is one of them. Her daughter-in-law Ruth is another. It's easy to see why Boaz had no real problem with the idea of marrying a Moabitess—even though his nearest kinsman did—if his mother was a foreigner.

In Rahab we see how the name can be a blessing down many generations. By contrast, Rehoboam also appears in Matthew's genealogy of Jesus, but we see in him just the opposite: the wasting of all entrusted to him.

The spirit Rachab, the dark guardian of the threshold in the immaterial realm, is a waster. As we approach a significant threshold, some of us try to avoid Python the Constrictor by placing ourselves in Rachab's hands instead.

While it promises to enlarge us, it actually spreads us so thin and subjects us to so much wasting, we feel compelled to back away from the open door. Maybe until we re-group and try again. Maybe forever.

Many people feel betrayed by God. However we don't fall accidentally into the hands of Rachab or Python. These are active choices. There's no ill-chance involved.

We may not know at a conscious level what a threshold requires but unconsciously we're fully aware of the spiritual dynamic involved:

from time immemorial, all thresholds require a sacrifice.

In the hope the Constrictor and Waster will allow us through, most of us decide we'll offer up the choicest delicacy we can think of: part of our destiny.

But Python and Rachab aren't satisfied with just a part. They want it all.

Rick found the perfect position for his talents in a fledgling start–up company. He was thrilled when he was invited to go into partnership. He got on well with his prospective partner. They not only shared the same vision and values but also the same wild and wacky sense of humour.

Of course, there was a sacrifice to be made—that goes without saying. However, Rick was willing to pay the price involved: he'd have to move to another country.

Rick sold up. His apartment, his car and his truck. He gave away his furniture, television and sound system, his refrigerator and even boxes of books as well as small items like his frypan and alarm clock. He was determined on a clean sweep. A new life, a new beginning.

Throwing over the final semester of his post–graduate university studies, he gave in his notice at his workplace and refused three plum job offers in the month that followed.

His excitement mounted. On the night before he was due to fly out, he celebrated by taking all his friends out to a restaurant for a farewell dinner.

They were in the middle of a set of mutually complimentary speeches when his phone rang. He took a moment to look at the text. It was from his new partner. 'Don't come,' it said. 'I've decided to go it alone.'

Rick threw up.

Rick's partner made a sacrifice to the guardians of the threshold. Rick was it. Quite apart from the broken social contract and ensuing destruction of relationship, there's a massive spiritual dynamic in play. It resonates so strongly in the spirit realm that, years later, it's possible—if you are particularly sensitive to threshold violations—to sense the ongoing echoes.

I'd gone to visit that eminent psychiatrist who'd asked people to look around the room and choose an item that resonated with them. I wanted to pose a question. As a teacher in the seventies, I felt many of my colleagues, along with many parents, drove students into rebellion through strict and unenforceable rules. Instead of guiding teenagers towards independence, they almost forced rebellious confrontation. My question was: 'What is the difference between independence and rebellion?'

He stared at me. 'I'll have to think about that. Come back in two weeks and I'll have figured it out.' On discovering I was an aspiring author, he gave me a book to read by one of his clients—a multi-award winning writer. 'It was his first book,' he informed me. 'Tell me what you think when you bring it back.'

In retrospect, I've wondered if it was a test. I'm not sure, if I'd come back and said it was just the sort of thing I wanted to write, he'd have answered my question. The book was the author's first foray into print and the means by which he'd gained entry into the publishing world. A threshold book.

The protagonist was a small, angry, weedy, dark-haired, half-Vietnamese, half-American boy who didn't know the identity of his father. As I was reading, I was overwhelmed by the feeling I knew the person on whom the character was based. But my friend Jon was neither small, weedy, dark-haired, nor half-Vietnamese, half-American. Nor was his father unknown.

Jon was a blond giant of Scandinavian extraction, gentle and softly-spoken—completely unlike the angry protagonist of the novel.

Still I couldn't shake the feeling. Despite the age difference—Jon was in his early twenties—the characterisation screamed at me: *this is Jon*. I was only able to break the obsessive thought when I finally realised it was impossible for the character to be Jon. The boy committed suicide towards the end and Jon was manifestly still very much alive.

I returned the book at the next appointment with the psychiatrist and said it wasn't really my sort of book. No other comment. We changed the subject and he told me: 'Rebellion is a unilateral declaration and independence is a bilateral agreement.'

Important as that information was to me back then, it was as nothing to the significance of what I'd been gifted through reading the novel.

Several years went by and I happened to be at a party with a group of English teachers. Jon was also there. In fact, he was sitting right next to me when the topic of award-winning books and famous authors came up. One particular author's most recent books were under discussion. I wondered if anyone there had ever read this writer's first book. *Now's my opportunity*, I thought. Fortunately I only got partway through my question, 'Has anyone ever read …?' when there was an interruption.

I didn't get to reveal the book's name or finish my query: *Do any of you think the protagonist is just like Jon?*

The interruption was from Jon himself. Rising abruptly, he announced the author we were discussing had been his English teacher and he'd never forgive him for the very book whose title I'd been about to mention. He left. It later transpired the discussion had brought on suicidal thoughts and, as a consequence, he'd admitted himself to hospital for several days.

It was a heart-stopping, skin-tingling moment when Jon stood up. He'd been *sacrificed*. That particular word sprang instantly to my mind. The author had kick-started his career, in some mysterious way beyond my comprehension, by sacrificing Jon.

How had I—impossibly—recognised him in that story, despite the massive level of mis-direction in the character description? For years I puzzled over this question, until I realised the residue of such a threshold sacrifice is simply immense in the spirit realm.

And if ever you've been a threshold sacrifice yourself, and you're still staked to the entranceway, you have the sensitivity to discern the resonance.

Generally all of us know instinctively that, as we approach a new beginning, a threshold sacrifice is required. However, most people aren't willing to sacrifice others; usually they sacrifice themselves.

This is just as wrong.

We are called to *make* a sacrifice, not to *be* a sacrifice.

Christ is made the sure foundation,
Christ the head and cornerstone,
Chosen by the Lord, and precious,
Binding all the church in one:
Holy Zion's help forever
And her confidence alone.

Urbs beata Hierusalem, 7th century
trans. John Mason Neale

To understand the consequences of threshold covenant violation, we first need to understand covenants. In particular we need to understand how destiny is inseparably woven into names and the covenant over them. In *God's Poetry*, there's a re–iterated point—that poetry is the most important aspect of the destiny God breathes into our names. A name's meaning is not always as important as its song.

It's in the song we should look for the specific nature of the covenant God wants to make with us through our names. The science of linguistics offers us the etymology of a name, the derivation of its roots and an analytic look at its syllables, but isn't always the best approach to understanding it as God sees it. From the beginning of Scripture there are multitudes of examples showing how lives were shaped as much by the poetry of a name as a meaning. In fact, the story of Abram is a salutary warning about trusting too much in etymology.

When El Shaddai appeared, He announced, '*Behold, my covenant is with you and you shall be the father of many nations. No longer shall your name be called Abram, but your name shall be Abraham, for I have made you a father of many nations.*' (Genesis 15:4–5 NKJV)

Consequently, almost all lexicons of Old Testament Hebrew declare Abraham is derived from 'ab', *father*, and 'hamon', *multitude*, and means *father of a multitude*.

There's actually a problem with this. The issue is recognised by the Jewish Encyclopedia and by Arie Uittenbogaard at Abarim Publications. There's an R unaccounted for.

The element at the end of Abram's new name is actually not 'hm' but 'rhm'—which doesn't mean *multitude* at all. In fact, no one knows what the meaning is; it's unique. The element does not occur anywhere else in Scripture. The Jewish Encyclopedia goes so far as to state, 'The form "Abraham" yields no sense in Hebrew.'

However, if we ditch etymology in favour of poetry and wordplay, we find something extraordinarily beautiful precisely matching what God says. '*Behold, my* ***covenant*** *is* ***with*** *you and you shall be the* ***father of many nations.***'

The element 'brh' is embedded in the Hebrew of Abraham's name. It is 'barah', the root of 'berith' meaning *to cut a covenant.* Thus in the overlap of *father*, 'ab', and 'hamon', *multitude*, is *covenant*, binding them both together.[25]

However, there's more to it than this. Let's play around with some of the Hebrew letters of Abraham's name: abrhm.

With them we can make words corresponding to these English forms:

- Ebru or Hebrew—a significant word in that Abraham was the first man to be known as a Hebrew
- Arba or Hebron—a significant word in that Abraham made his name covenant with God at Hebron, passage, which was originally called Arba, four
- Barak or abrak—a significant word set in that the first means

blessing and the second *I will bless*, spelling out the prophetic destiny of Abraham as a blessing to all peoples through the cutting of this covenant

So, the statement 'The form "Abraham" yields no sense in Hebrew' is only true in etymological terms. God's magnificent poetry is enfolded within the name Abraham: *father of a multitude, covenant–cutter, Hebrew, passage, four*.

And not even that last possibility is overlooked in God's vigilance.

Four covenants are mentioned in quick succession in the story of Abraham. Many scholars recognise just two and are uncertain why the original covenant was repeated. They don't see any difference between the pair they recognise. Some, however, believe this demonstrates the editorial work of much–later writers. In my opinion, that is to miss their distinctively different nature.

- The first is a blood covenant.
- The second is a name covenant.
- The third is a threshold covenant.
- The fourth is a salt covenant.

These cover the four major types of covenants of ancient times. I have discussed the first two so extensively in *God's Poetry* and *God's Panoply* I will only briefly mention some of the important details here.

The purpose of a covenant ceremony is not primarily to solemnise a contract. This significant aspect of it is often misunderstood as the main reason for the ritual. The commercial aspects of an agreement or bargain are completely overshadowed by the true purpose of covenant: oneness.

Covenant is to restore what was lost in Eden: humanity's oneness with God and with each other.

In later times a blood covenant was a sevenfold rite incorporating name and salt covenants as well. However, as described in Genesis

15:9–21, it simply involved the sacrifice of three animals and two birds and the walk of blood.

It was unusual to have three sacrificial animals. Normally there was only one. So here is one of the first hints of God's Trinitarian nature.

In a blood covenant ceremony, it was normal to sacrifice a goat, bull or lamb and cut it in half down the centre. The pieces were placed on the ground a short distance apart with a puddle of blood in the middle.

Abram sacrificed a three-year old heifer, a three-year old goat and a three-year old ram and divided them in half. He also sacrificed a dove and a pigeon but did not divide them.

After nightfall, the Lord appears to participate in the walk of blood. At this time, Abram does not know Him as El Shaddai. It will be another fourteen years before that revelation.

In an ordinary blood covenant ceremony, the participants would walk around the pieces in a figure ∞ (and given the everlasting nature of covenants, this is now, very appropriately, a symbol of infinity). They would then stop in the blood puddle to pronounce blessings and curses.

The curses were simple: if either of us violates this covenant, we deserve death, just as this animal has died.

The blessings were equally simple: we will give our lives for each other, just as this animal has given its life.

In Abram's story, the blessings went even further, including a promise his descendants would inherit the land many centuries in the future. Some curses were implied. And perhaps there is an implied weapon exchange when God says right at the start well before the ceremony is undertaken: *'I am your shield, your very great reward.'* (Genesis 15:1 NIV)

The exchange of belts (with all their associated weapons) was meant to symbolise the promise: *everything I have is yours. I will defend you to the death. Your enemies are now my enemies. I will protect you and yours as I would protect my own.*

There is no indication that either of the other exchanges (coats and names), which became normal in later times, actually took place on this occasion. Indeed, since the second covenant between God and Abram is specifically about names, it seems the other exchanges did not occur for at least another fourteen years.

The immediate prelude to that second covenant is the sudden appearance of God, announcing His own name. It's not the one He would give to Moses at the burning bush half a millennium later. Nor the one Joshua would learn during a battle with the Amalekites. Nor the one David would learn defending sheep from lions and bears.

It is El Shaddai*, the Lord Almighty*—the first of seven covenant names—which has a sense of 'the all–sufficient One', 'the One–who–is–more–than–enough'.

Still, even that doesn't get to the root of it. The fundamental meaning of 'Shaddai' is obscured by all these polished renderings.

Just as Jesus weeping over Jerusalem and likening Himself to a hen with her chicks has strong motherly overtones, the first of God's covenant names has quite clear–cut maternal implications. Its most basic meaning is *the strong–breasted one*. The nurturer. The one who cherishes, who cares, who feeds, who protects, who stands in harm's way, who comforts.

Very few of these nuances come across with the usual translation: *the Lord Almighty.*

The name covenant exchange between Abram, Sarai and El Shaddai symbolised the death of individuality: '*It is no longer "I" who live, but "we"*'. The participants became in effect one heart beating in two bodies.

Even today, a remnant of this tradition persists. We still hark back to name covenants when, during a wedding ceremony, a bride takes on her husband's name.

By the end of the name covenant described in Genesis 17, Abram and Sarai are Abraham and Sarah.

Abram, *exalted father*, has become Abraham, usually translated *father of a multitude* (though we've already noted it has *covenant* and *four* in it too).

Sarai, *princess*, has become Sarah, *princess*.

Odd, you may think. Nothing's happened to the meaning of Sarah's name. Her identity has undergone a radical shift, however.

Both Abraham and Sarah had an 'h' added to their name. Today such a change of spelling is held as insignificant. In rabbinic understanding, however, 'h' was shorthand for HaShem, *the Name*. HaShem was itself shorthand for the sacred not-to-be-spoken Name of God.

In cutting a name covenant with God, His name became an integral part of theirs.

Most people today know nothing about name covenants, what it means when you assume someone else's name, change your name or adopt a pseudonym.

Just what will our lives look like, if our names are not one with Jesus Christ? What happens when they are instead one with the names of other gods?

Alison wanted to come into her destiny, so she asked me what her name meant.

I believe most names have been so sanitised over the centuries that, the older a name is, the more its mythic content will have been whitewashed. Generally speaking, the average book or website list offers a meaning that is, at best, a vague guide. And at worst—the total opposite. Even Hebrew lexicons can succumb to the imperative for a micro-definition which, as we have just seen in the case of Abraham, leaves out major aspects.

Nevertheless, despite the challenges presented by name dictionaries, I also believe every individual knows, deep within, what their name truly means. And there's a way to find it out: *dreams*.

God tells us, over and over, in our dreams.

'My instinct says it's Welsh,' I told Alison. 'However, every book I consult suggests Alice from Old French, Aalis, allegedly a short form of Adelaide from Adalheidis, *noble kind*. You don't really want to know what 'heid' means, so tell me your recurring dream.'

As far as I'm concerned, a recurring dream—especially one lasting from childhood through to adulthood—is God speaking directly to you about your destiny. Therefore, it's about your name.

And that's what Alison was really asking me. Not: 'What does my name mean?' But: 'What is God calling me to? What is the purpose for which I was put here on earth?'

But when she revealed her recurring dream, I was baffled. 'It's just a child,' she said. 'A child, alone and silent.'

Hmm ... that doesn't sound like Alice or Adelaide.

'I think,' Alison went on, 'it's a part of myself I need to get in touch with.'

That could be right, I thought. *Maybe this recurring dream is not about her name at all. Ahh, well, nice theory while it lasted.*

For over a year, I investigated Alice and Adelaide. I dug into the background of French 'Aalis' and discovered a faint possibility it meant *rowan tree.* With that in mind, I momentarily considered Alison might be a variant of Lisa. Then I found 'aliso' is Spanish for the *alder tree.* So I asked Alison again about her recurring dreams, hoping she'd mention a tree.

But she always came back to the child.

Child, Alice ... *nothing.*

However, she also said she'd once had a vision of pink roses.

Roses, child, Alice ... *nothing.*

'Alison' soon became, by far, the most difficult name I'd ever investigated. I was ready to concede defeat but, before I did, I asked for more detail about the child. *What was the child wearing? Holding? What did she look like?*

Alison answered that her age varied from a baby to a toddler. She was very fair. The only thing all the dreams had in common was she was always *in* something. The first time she appeared was as a baby in a basket.

Baby in a basket? Two names immediately sprang to mind: Moses and Taliesin.[26]

The first was easily dismissed. The second rhymed with Alison.

Could it really be? God is a poet and we are God's poetry, as Ephesians 2:10 says, but would He totally by-pass the root meaning in favour of a rhyme? The only real difference in sound between Alison and Taliesin is the initial letter. Sure there are many prophetic examples of rhymes and assonance determining destiny in Scripture—but most of them refer to the names of towns.

Taliesin is a Welsh name, going back over fifteen hundred years, and meaning *radiant brow* or *fair brow.*

While the meaning would account for the fairness of the child in Alison's dream, there was a big problem. Taliesin was the chief bard of the Old North. As far as I was concerned, the name evoked harps, music and golden-throated song. In some legends, he is confused and conflated with Merlin. His story, *Hanes Taliesin*, begins, '*My original country is the region of the summer stars ...*' and mixes myth and history in almost equal proportions.

I'd known Alison for over twenty years and, if her name was truly related to the god-like Taliesin, she should be a composer and a singer—a musician of towering, incomparable talent.

However, I couldn't recall her ever mentioning any musical gift whatsoever.

I should have remembered her roses: a symbol of secrecy from ancient times.

I decided to test the waters on the 'Alison-is-derived-from-Taliesin' theory.[27] 'If you could have your choice of any musical instrument,' I asked, 'what would you learn?'

'Oboe, maybe clarinet.'

Well, that shoots the theory down in flames. 'Not a harp?' I asked.

'At $90 a string?' Alison retorted.

I'll just resurrect that theory. How many people know the price of a harp string?

Alison turned out to have staggering musical talent—a gift she'd put aside in her late teens, deciding not to enter the conservatorium.

As we prayed to restore Alison's identity and destiny, I remembered the 'heid' of Adelaide. It lurked in the background of Taliesin's story too. 'Heid' is an old Norse word meaning *black magic*.

The problem was evident: Alison's name needed re-consecration to Jesus. The covenant over it—its essential oneness—was with a Welsh demi-god. And when your spirit knows it, as hers did, there is conflict between your soul and your spirit. Your heart is divided against itself.

Music ... can name the unnameable and communicate the unknowable.

Leonard Bernstein

Who is your name dedicated to?

That may sound like an odd question, whatever your Christian tradition.[28] If you were given a baptismal name as an infant, then the ceremony itself should ensure your name was dedicated to God. Shouldn't it?

Or if you became a Christian later in life, then surely your decision for Christ would cover the dedication of your name. Wouldn't it?

Isn't 'it', as the pastor in the story about Steve that Gordon Dalbey related, 'all done at the cross'?

This cliché is so often raised it's worth examining in some detail. What exactly is 'it'? And what, more importantly, is 'it' *not*?

The Cross of Jesus is about salvation: not just for heaven but for our time on earth as well. For Christians, the three ordinary exchanges of a covenant take on supernatural overtones when Jesus is involved: life instead of death, defence instead of opposition, membership of God's family instead of spiritual exile.

Nothing we can do can ever earn salvation. Nothing we can do can ever add to or take away from what Jesus achieved. It is God's gift. His lavish extension of grace. End of story.

However, let's make a careful distinction here. Confusion arises when we lump salvation and calling together as an indefinite 'it' which was dealt with, once and for all, at the Cross. Salvation is the stunning and magnificent precursor to being enabled to come into our calling; it has absolutely nothing to do with us and everything to do with the Cross of Jesus. It is foundational to becoming a co-worker with God (and if that notion surprises you, take a good look at 1 Corinthians 3:9) and using our talents as He always intended. He has plans for us which go back to before we were born, but He won't force us to follow them.

In contrast to salvation, when it comes to our calling, there's quite a lot up to us. We're supposed to be yoked to Jesus but we can choose to take no risks, bury our talents and thereby take away from God's kingdom. Although our salvation is secure, we will be judged according to how we used our talents, along with the evidence of the fruit of the Spirit in our lives.

The notion that Christians can simply forget the past and put it entirely behind them because it has no more power to harm is only partly true. Any event from the past which is still negatively affecting the present is not truly 'past' at all; it is alive and well and needs to be intentionally taken to the cross of Jesus and there put to death.

Name covenants can be part of this unredeemed personal—or family—history. Sometimes it's simple to identify the spirit presiding over the dedication within a name covenant and affecting an individual's calling. Sometimes it's not so easy.

But the fact is, if you seek, you will find. The door will be opened. But it's necessary to seek diligently and to check out the poetry as well as the meaning: the rhymes, the assonances, the puns, the cognates.

Because God is a poet as Ephesians 2:10 tells us—*For we are His poetry, created in Christ Jesus for good works, which He prepared beforehand that we should walk in them.*[29]

You may think the notion God loves puns and poetry more than meaning is almost a sacrilegious idea. Yet Scripture is full of wordplay. Some of the humour is glitteringly clever but some is a matter for head–scratching. Still, it doesn't seem appropriate to groan aloud as God banters with His prophets.

'What do you see?' He asks Jeremiah.

'An almond tree.'

'You're right! I'm watching over My word to activate My promises.'

It seems a completely random reply in English, but it's built around a pun on the Hebrew word for *almond* tree: 'shaqed'. The word for *watching*, 'shaqad', sounds just like it.

This is not an isolated case.

'What do you see?' He asks Amos.

'A basket of summer fruit.'

'You're right! The end has come upon my people, Israel.'

Amos' reply and God's rejoinder are based around another pun: *summer fruit*, 'qayits', and *end*, 'qets'.

When I was in my late teens I hung around a group where the boys loved verbal jousting. They kept careful score in their pun competitions and were always trying to top each other. These games irritated me.

So, to discover God likes puns enough to tell His prophets the destiny of places through them, as He does for the nine towns described by Micah, was quite disconcerting.[30] I was hoping it was an aberration, but I realised it wasn't when I went back to Genesis and looked at Adam's name. It's a pun—a multi–level pun, in fact, on *red* and *dust* and *ground*.

I just knew that, if things started this way from the beginning, they weren't going to change. And they don't.

Consider, for instance, that well–known title for Jesus: 'the Lamb of God'. In Hebrew, 'tale'' means both *lamb* and *youth*. It's basically both *young man* and *young sheep*. It lends a whole new level of resonance to the passages where God's people are likened to sheep and to the Lord as the Good Shepherd.

Consider also the name Israel.

Several meanings are given for it: *prince with God* or *God strives* or *the one who struggles with God*. In the context of his acquisition of the name—the midnight wrestle with God's shaliach[31]—any of these could make sense.

But it's rare to find a mention of the exceedingly revealing nature of this: whatever it actually means, it's also a pun on his grandmother's name.

Sarai means *princess*. When God undertook a name covenant with Abram and his wife, they became Abraham and Sarah. Abram's name changed in meaning but Sarai's didn't. Sarah still meant *princess*, derived from 'sar', *prince*. However, both Sarah and Abraham had the same new letter included in their names: 'h'.

In a name covenant, the participants receive each other's names: God takes the names *exalted father* and *prince* and offers Abram and Sarai, in exchange, His own. According to rabbinical commentary, God's name is symbolised by 'h' for HaShem, *the name*. As 'h' is shorthand for HaShem, so HaShem itself is shorthand for the *Name of God*.[32]

So Sarai might mean *princess* but Sarah is, more accurately, *princess with God*.

When her grandson Jacob is renamed Israel, *prince with God*, he comes into a new destiny—just as Sarai did when she became Sarah, *princess with God*.[33]

However, until I became aware these two names had a common base, I'd missed noticing how alike Jacob and Sarah were. They were both consummate and inveterate schemers. Neither of them particularly cared whom they hurt or used in the process of getting what they wanted. Nor did either of them really trust God to usher them into their destiny without considerable help on their part.

The trickle of scheming and favouritism starting with Sarah flowed down the generational stream until, by the time of Joseph, it became a flood in full spate. Joseph's brothers came up with a scheme involving attempted murder, human trafficking and grand–scale deception.

Sow the wind in one generation, reap the whirlwind a few later.

True for both blessings and curses.

And when it comes to blessing, this connection between Jacob and his grandmother might account for one of the most mysterious titles in all Scripture: the House of Jacob.

Then Moses went up to God, and the Lord called to him from the mountain and said, 'This is what you are to say to the house of Jacob and … tell the people of Israel: "You yourselves have seen what I did to Egypt … Now if you obey Me fully and keep My covenant, then … you will be My treasured possession … "'

Exodus 19:3–6 NIV

According to some rabbis, the House of Jacob in this passage is not synonymous with the people of Israel. It's not the usual poetic parallelism. They identify the House of Jacob as specifically referring to 'the women of the tribes of Israel' and suggest the text indicates that, at Mount Sinai, the women stepped forward first to accept the covenant of the Law. The Israelite men, still smarting over the golden calf, were slow to follow that lead.

Yechiel Eckstein points out nuances in the following which are not usually conveyed in English: *All who were willing, men and women alike, came and brought gold jewelry of all kinds: brooches, earrings, rings and ornaments. They all presented their gold as a wave offering to the Lord.* (Exodus 35:22 NIV) In Hebrew, the verse more literally reads: '*The men came on the heels of the women.*' The women had refused to give up their gold ornaments to be melted down for the golden calf but they were first in line to give them for God's tabernacle. The men had given Moses up for dead but the women were steadfast in waiting for his return from the mountain.[34]

Fast–forward a few thousand years and it's the men who give Jesus up for dead but the women who remain steadfast and maintain a vigil at the foot of the Cross.

Fast-forward another couple of thousand years again and look around our churches today. Not much has changed.

Much as I hate to admit it, I've not only overcome my irritation with puns, I'm now like those annoying boys I once knew. I rate the puns in Scripture as to their quality.

Isaiah's prophecy about Jerusalem, which I used to think quite fine, is now just fair to middling. The words rely on the similarity of *lion* and *altar hearth* in Hebrew. Ariel, *lion*, had been the name of David's citadel in Zion and Isaiah uses it to prophesy the fate of Jerusalem as 'arieyl', *an altar hearth*. The idea is an *ash heap*; a modern connotation would be *holocaust*.

Micah does a roll-call of eight towns and prophesies their destiny, using a repertoire of poetic devices—rhyme, assonance and allusion—as well as straightforward meaning. For instance, his prophecy about the town of Ophrah, which means *a fawn*, relies on the assonance, 'aphrah', *dust*.

There's some really clever wordplay involved but these examples pale in comparison with a couple of surpassing brilliance found in the New Testament writings.

Jesus of Nazareth had exceptional poetic talent and so did Paul of Tarsus. You didn't know Jesus wrote poetry? That he composed dazzling, accomplished verse?

That's one of the problems of forgetting the gospels in their original Greek form are *already* translations.[35] If God is a poet as Ephesians 2:10 testifies, then Jesus must also have been a superlative wordsmith. So why aren't we aware of this?

Simple.

Poetry is notoriously the first casualty of literary translations, so it should be no surprise to realise the jewelled Aramaic verse of Jesus has simply disappeared in the Greek rendering. Occasionally it can be recaptured.

Ken Bailey quotes from a parable Jesus told—that of a servant's inability to bow to two masters, God and mammon—from an Aramaic text used in the twentieth century in churches throughout the Middle East.[36] It's verse so intricate and profound, it makes perfect sense why the disciples so readily recalled the words of Jesus years later. The features of his poetry gave it the quality of being easily remembered.

Paul of Tarsus ended his epistle to the Ephesians with a poetic rhapsody about armour, armour-bearing, love, forgiveness and submission—by which, I have argued in *God's Panoply*, he actually meant *uplift*—and a sevenfold pageant of mathematics and song, as well as a covenant kiss.

It's so rich and complex that, although I took a long, significant look at it in *God's Panoply*, I've barely scratched the surface.

Curiously, both Jesus' and Paul's most intricate wordplay involves thresholds. Perhaps that's because they're such complicated places. In the physical world they have lintels, posts, doors, hinges, locks, keys and sweeps. In the spiritual realm, a covenant, a cornerstone, seals and a mezuzah—a symbolic 'keeper of memory'—should be added. Not to mention threshold guardians.

Yet despite this almost incomparable complexity, in today's world we're likely to think of them as nothing more than doorways.

It is not the mountain that we conquer but ourselves.

Sir Edmund Hillary

Hagar had given God a name. Out in the desert, fleeing from her mistress, pregnant with her master's son, she'd encountered an Angel of the Lord. Hagar was miserable and desperate. An Egyptian bondservant, she had probably been acquired during the time Abram and Sarai were down around the Nile River. She may have even been given to them by Pharaoh, when he was trying to make amends after discovering Sarai was not just Abram's half-sister but his wife.

Hagar's experience with the angel revealed to her that God is outstandingly compassionate. She therefore gave God a name: 'the One Who sees'. Later, when her son was born, she named him Ishmael because God also hears.

Ishmael, Simeon, Samuel are all taken from the same root: *to hearken, to hear and obey, to listen and do.*

For the Hebrews, listening was an action that automatically resulted in a reaction. It wasn't inert in the way we conceive of it today.

On the other hand, perhaps I malign the contemporary world—obviously passive listening was a problem even two millennia ago. James, the head of the church in Jerusalem, had to spell it out: '*Don't, I beg you, only hear the message, but put it into practice; otherwise you are merely deluding yourselves.*' (James 1:22, JB Phillips)

For the Jews, listening meant acting on what was heard. Not so for the Greeks. It was obvious James had immense difficulty getting this concept across to the Greek-influenced Christians because he also had to explain the indivisibility of listening and doing: '*But some will say: "You have faith and I have works." Show me your faith apart from your works and I by my works will show you my faith.*' (James 2:18 RSV)

In fact, he then immediately engaged in some serious butt-kicking: '*You believe that there is one God? Good! Even the demons do that—and shudder.*' (James 2:19 NIV)

Martin Luther so loathed these remarks he called the letter of James an 'epistle of straw'. But our world is so deeply imbued with Greek thinking we need James' stern warnings that faith is not mentally assenting to the right theological doctrines. It's not a belief in the head without any power to move the heart and spill out in right action.

Faith is an active verb.

Like love.

James wraps up his argument about faith and works by pointing to Abraham, the friend of God.

Abraham of course had also given God a name, a considerable time after Hagar had: his expression for God is famous as Jehovah Jireh, *the Lord Who provides*, even though 'Yireh' is more correctly rendered as *the One Who sees.*

He agrees with Hagar—thirty, perhaps even fifty years later. In between the two times God was dubbed 'the One Who sees', He Himself announced His own name: El Shaddai.

The announcement was His overture to the name covenant with Abram and Sarai. He enfolded their names so they became 'Abraham' and 'Sarah'.

A few days later—three days in rabbinical literature; six, in my view—He turned up again, this time with an angelic escort.

A little unusual. When He cut the previous two covenants, El Shaddai hadn't brought company. Now He had a pair of guards by His side.

Not just one angel was in evidence. Two were.

Their appearance at this juncture is highly significant. A duo of angelic sentinels is a signature element indicating a threshold covenant.

From the cherubim at the gates of Eden to the angels guarding the stone door at the tomb of Joseph of Arimathea, their appearance signifies not only a spiritual threshold but extreme peril.[37]

In fact, the lurking danger has potentially fatal consequences for the unwary. Whatever God does, Satan mimics. Not all of the threshold guardians mentioned in Scripture are on the side of light, goodness and truth. As the cherubim are appointed by God to watch over thresholds, so Python and Rachab fulfil the same role on behalf of hell.

Going back to the story of Abraham, this is why, in my view, God brought in the cherubim as heavy-duty protection. God doesn't need protection—these angels were there to defend Abraham *and his family*. And that family happened to include his nephew Lot.

When God instituted the supreme threshold covenant—the Passover—He took that protection to a whole new level. But that was to be quite a few centuries in the future.

Now a few days previously Abraham had just got his new name. He was sitting in the doorway of his tent, probably feeling distinctly uncomfortable. He'd been circumcised at the age of 100.

He spotted some travellers coming towards him and, just as

the traditionally hospitable Bedouins still do today, he leapt up to welcome them.

As Henry Clay Trumbull noted, a threshold covenant was simply part of the normal hospitality practices of ancient times. When a stranger appeared at a tent or in a village, seeking shelter and food, any individual of noble character would consider it an honour to take him in as a guest and undertake threshold rites: in effect, a 'temporary' covenant.

Normally covenants are forever. They bring the participants into oneness: two minds, one heart; two bodies, one soul.

Trumbull further points out that, if a householder actually knew a guest was due, he would display signs of welcome: blood on the lintel and doorposts, dripping down onto the cornerstone. This signified the fatted calf had been killed and the guest was invited not only to a feast but to become part of the family.

If the guest accepted the invitation, he would carefully step across the cornerstone. He would 'pass over' the threshold. If the guest declined the invitation, intending to insult the householder, he would trample on the cornerstone.

God, for the first time, comes to His friend's home: He *passes over* the threshold.

Ordinarily, when two men undertook this temporary covenantal oneness, they would enter into certain obligations with each other. They were committed to protect each other for the duration of the visit and also for a reasonable period afterwards. They became each other's covenant defender.

This was true even if, under normal circumstances, they were bitter foes. If an enemy turned up, seeking sanctuary, a man of noble character would neither hesitate to provide it, nor fail to protect him if needed.

Perhaps this is why Abraham is so bold in asking God to spare Sodom—he's trading on grace while the opportunity presents itself.

Not, of course, that Abraham's is a temporary covenant. The salt covenant, if not the previously undertaken blood and name covenants, ensured that this was forever.

The saying, 'There is bread and salt between us,' which has been prevalent in the East from time immemorial, is equal to saying, 'We are bound together by a solemn covenant.' ... A noble foe refuses to 'taste the salt' of his adversary—that is, to eat with him—so long as he feels disinclined to be reconciled with him. Such a foe dreads the thought of repudiating the covenant which the breaking of bread together forms.

Abraham Mitrie Rihbany, *The Syrian Christ*

Henry Clay Trumbull suggested we've been misled about the first Passover. He maintained threshold covenants haven't changed in millennia and, in failing to understand them, we've inverted the nature of the Passover. Blood dripping down lintels and doorposts was a well-known welcome sign hosts would display to honour their visitors. It signalled the feast was prepared and the host was only awaiting the guest's arrival to begin.

Trumbull's contention was the blood on the Passover threshold was never intended to deter the Angel of Death. Rather it was a banner proclaiming, 'Welcome, Lord!' It announced an offer of hospitality to God Himself, similar to Abraham's. It celebrated God's arrival with a feast and delighted in His presence as a covenant defender.

The Hebrew word, 'pesach', from which we derive the adjective 'paschal' for *Easter*, is thought to mean *leap* or *hop* or *pass over*.

'Pass over' the cornerstone is exactly what a guest did when he accepted a host's invitation. The first Passover of God therefore refers to the Lord accepting the Israelites' invitation and entering their houses by passing over the sacred cornerstones.

I find it fascinating that, in the seventeenth century—the era when religious iconography was banned by law in many parts of Europe, along with references to God in stories and poetry—there is the abrupt appearance of a seasonal image like the Easter Bunny. Despite attempts to give the egg-dispensing rabbit a long and respectable pagan heritage, it actually first appears in Germany as the Osterhase about three centuries ago.

I'm suspicious: 'Os' after all is an ancient Teutonic word for *god*. Perhaps Os in Osterhase is an allusion to a pagan god but I find it doubtful. I don't know of any gods who leap, spring, hop or otherwise pass over a threshold other than the God of Israel.

Furthermore, if I lived in a time when it was forbidden by law to refer directly to God but yet wanted to discuss the God who passes over, I'd be hard put to choose a better symbol than a rabbit or a hare.[38]

This failure to understand the nature of threshold covenant may have meant we've attributed pagan origins to what is very likely an innovative Christian symbol. Still, it's by no means the most significant loss which has occurred because we no longer take any account of threshold or the covenants that govern them.

My mum had to pick up a parcel one day in the centre of the city. As she parked her car, she noticed a shabby man in a shiny wheelchair in the gutter further up the street. As she went off to get the parcel, she felt a mounting sense of anger. Who would have left a helpless man dangling off the side of a busy road like that?

Ten minutes later, she was back at her car, the parcel in her hands. To her dismay, the man was still there. How could hundreds of passers-by have ignored his plight? She got in her car, switched on the ignition and started to leave. Then she stopped and re-parked it.

She went up to the man and noticed he was dressed in a decrepit old suit. One of his legs was missing and the right front of his pants was rolled up and fastened with a massive safety pin. 'Are you ok?' she asked.

Now it so happened the wheelchair was parked adjacent to my

dad's workplace. My mum's big concern was that his boss would appear while she was there. As she looked around, sure enough there was dad's boss, staring at her.

She was the type of executive wife about whom one of his colleagues remarked at a party, 'Hamilton, I realise you must only have one wife because, if you had any other, you'd have brought it.'

She didn't fit into the almost-dilettante workplace social scene at all.

By this time, she didn't particularly care about her reputation sliding further. She'd established that Toby really did need help. He wanted to get to the wheelchair-accessible toilet block in a park some distance away. With only one leg, he couldn't negotiate the toilets nearby.

Mum started to push him there. As soon as they reached the park, several homeless people took an interest. 'G'day, Toby. You right?'

'Hey, Toby, you ok today?'

'Need a hand, Toby?'

'Nar,' he said to the giant Afro-American asking the last question. 'A *lady* is taking me today.'

All the time they'd headed for the toilets, Toby had told my mum his life story. He even mentioned that his nephew, who had just bought him his new wheelchair, was the person who had left him in the gutter. But that wasn't a worry as far as he was concerned—someone always came to his rescue. His friends who lived in the park were always looking out for him.

Mum started to panic as they neared the toilets. How would he manage?

But the toilets were built for people with disabilities and there were friends there to help him.

At the entrance, she said, 'Goodbye.'

'One last favour,' Toby said.

'Yes?'

'Come to the front of the chair. I want to see your face.'

For the first time, my mum began to be suspicious.

'I have to stand before the Lord very soon.' He took her hand and kissed it. 'And when I do I want to remember your face so I can describe you to Him.'

My mum has never forgotten Toby because of his final words to her.

And she's often wondered who he really was. Even at the time, the situation was bizarre but, in retrospect, the story of a nephew who cared enough to buy a shiny brand new wheelchair but not enough to leave his uncle in a safe place was a little too weird.

Was Toby really a shabby one–legged old man? Was he an angel on assignment? Or was he someone more unusual still—one of heaven's councillors?

Every action of our lives touches on some chord that will vibrate in eternity.

Edwin Hubell Chapin

There's something quite odd in the story of God turning up with two angels to visit Abraham: the timing. It had been fourteen years since God had cut a blood covenant with Abram. How long had it been since the institution of the name covenant? A week at most.

Surely the Lord of time could have spaced these events out better—you know, seven years and seven years has something significantly 'seven–ish' to recommend them.

Is there a rush? Or does that name covenant move more in the heavenlies than is obvious?

In the story of Haimona, there's a clue why God moves so quickly to institute a third covenant once the second is in place.

When Haimona stepped onto the threshold of destiny, the primary attack on him was directed against his name. Destiny is encoded in name[39] so to send in a spiritual bombardment against a name is the same as launching a strike against an individual's destiny.

Perhaps this is why Abraham's threshold covenant with God happened just a few days after he'd received a new name. The destiny God had always promised him was imminent. If there were to be a demonic strike which would affect every nation on earth for generations to come, the days immediately following the name covenant were the most crucial.

Haimona's story wasn't just about the spiritual forces arraigned against him. It was also about his complicity in his own defeat: his own long-established vows used against him. As his own worst enemy, he was on the side of the forces trying to destroy him. He self-sabotaged.

This, to a lesser extent, is also true in the story of Alison. Her vows and judgments came into play: it transpired she resented her parents' sacrifice of themselves to ensure she had all the opportunities they'd missed out on. On the verge of a brilliant career in music, she threw it all in. Complicit with the spirit of wasting, she perpetuated the very thing she hated in her parents: hasty sacrifice.

Alison isn't the only person I've encountered like this. Another woman had talent so vast that, in every music examination from Year 1 to 7, she scored in the top three in the entire world. Yet she abysmally failed her final entry examination to college.

I'm the president of a writing club: I cannot begin to count the number of people who spend years of their lives—thousands of hours—writing a book but fail to spend two minutes googling the reputation of the company asking them for money to subsidise that book's publication. The most heart-wrenching message I've ever received was from a member who decided never to write again: 'If God wanted me to be an author, He wouldn't have allowed me to be trapped by a vanity publisher four times in the past year.'

Yet, I'd pointed her to warnings on the internet twelve months previously about the ethics of that particular company. It wasn't that she hadn't prayed. She'd simply been deaf to any negative comments. When we become deaf, to either negative or positive comments, we put ourselves into the hands of a very specialised group of Python's allies: the 'sons of pride'.

Many people self-sabotage just as the door opens wide for their talent. So many people are ready to make the sacrifice that coming into their destiny requires but are thrown back as the door slams viciously shut.

God seems to have called us, then abandoned us. We've experienced patterns of constriction or wasting or both ... time and time again. We've had opportunities to engage with our destiny but, when we've tried, we've had the life throttled out of us—or else we've encountered financial or material wasting.

How do we understand this?

How can we possibly understand why God fails to protect us at this critical moment? Doesn't the whole of Scripture testify He is our shield, our defender, our very great reward?

Is He testing us?

If so, the tests are so hard many people despair, they give up, they chase a lesser dream—some even lose their faith entirely.

At one point, Alison applied for a job in a primary school as a teacher aide. We were still working on the meaning of her name at that time and, in her delight at obtaining the position, she said, 'I don't feel I faced any constriction or wasting at all. I was almost offered this on a platter.'

'But is it your calling?' I asked her.

At the time, she seemed to think so. And indeed, if her calling was to be a teacher aide, then there was no sacrifice at all. However if, as we came to see, her calling is to be a composer of innovative worship music, then that's an entirely different story.

Many of us have put our dreams so far behind us, we've even forgotten they ever existed. We've thrust our buoyant youthful hopes aside for the realism of maturity.

'Realism'?

The truth, for those of us who shoot ourselves in the foot every time we approach the open door, is that we recognise the threshold guardians—the principalities of constriction and wasting—and we sacrifice a part of ourselves, hoping it will be enough to appease them.

But, as we might suspect, it never is.

... the idea of the zebihat *[is one] with which the West is not familiar. The ... host honoured his guest most highly by killing a sheep at the threshold of the house, upon the guest's arrival, and inviting him to step over the blood into the house. This act formed a 'blood covenant' between the guest and his host. It made them one.*

Abraham Mitrie Rihbany, *The Syrian Christ*

A few days after Abram undertook a name covenant and became Abraham, God arrived to finally solve the biggest problem of his name. What was this problem? Fatherhood.

Abraham not only had issues with becoming a father, he had issues with his own father. As it happens, both these issues can be summed up in a single word: *delay*.

Terah, *delay*, was his father's name.

Did Abram make a choice between abba Terah and Abba El Shaddai? Did honouring one mean dishonouring the other?[40] I have to suspect so. Despite Abram's belief in God being counted to him as righteousness, it's obvious he still had major problems around delay.

Having a son by Hagar might not have been his idea but he was completely complicit in Sarai's plan. Delay was undoubtedly an even bigger issue for her, when it came to the crunch.[41]

So it seems God recognised the potential problems with another delay: the likelihood Abraham would sabotage his new destiny if He didn't step in. The fact is *delay* and *father* had both been entwined in

Abraham's mind from the moment he was born. He'd already created future problems for all who would one day call themselves 'Children of Abraham': Jew and Arab alike.

His contemporary, Job, would become renowned for his patience but, virtuous as Abraham was, forbearance was not his strong point. If you think this comment is a little harsh, I'd like to point out that, after Sarah died, he had six sons by Keturah and they were the ancestors of tribes who later became (and still remain) enemies of the Israelites.

So God's prompt appearance forestalls additional disaster at this point. Note the two angels accompanying Him are eventually revealed as warrior guardians. They weren't messengers but protectors.

The appearance of a pair of angels is the first hint there's a threshold covenant underway. A second hint is given in the description of Abraham's instinctive response to the situation: he acts as a good host and invites the strangers to a meal. He washes their feet, orders bread to be baked, kills a calf and prepares it while serving them milk and curds: we're not talking fast-food takeout here. These are the traditional elements of a meal to accompany a blood covenant.

Bishop KC Pillai discusses the giving of milk in the context of Jael's hospitality to Sisera: as there wasn't any refrigerator to keep it cool, it would have had to have been buttermilk, tied up in a milkskin and prepared with salt to keep it from spoiling. It's subtle but unmistakeable: here is the fourth covenant—that of salt.

A salt covenant is everlasting in nature; it's a pledge of unbreakable faithfulness, a promise of eternal fidelity. A person of integrity who dined with another where food seasoned with salt has been eaten ought never betray or harm the other. (Herein lies the seriousness of Judas' betrayal and the significance of Jesus' words about sharing the same dish. Though, in more recent times, it's regarded as wise to dine frequently if you are worried someone might turn against you: it's said that, for scoundrels, the salt must still be in their belly for the covenant to hold.)

In the past in the Middle East, it was customary on the last day of the bridal week for salt to be brought and for the couple to place some on their tongues, saying: 'In the name of the salt, I agree to do all that

I have promised, so help me God.' This is the origin of the wedding breakfast: to eat food prepared with salt.

During the threshold covenant God undertook with Abraham and Sarah, He promised them a son when the 'time of life' was up. Some translations render 'time of life' as 'a year' or 'next year'—*'I will establish my covenant with Isaac, whom Sarah shall bear to you at this time next year.'* (Genesis 17:21 ESV)

However, this promise and fulfilment foreshadows the conception and birth of the Church. Jesus renamed Simon as Cephas, *threshold rock*, on Yom Kippur, the Day of Atonement. 'Kippur', like 'cephas', is a threshold-related word. The birth of the church at Pentecost fulfils Jesus' threshold promise: 'on this rock I will build My Church.' Because, as we shall see, the parallel is so strong, and because Pentecost is around nine months after Yom Kippur, I believe that the 'time of life' is simply the period of human gestation.

Now Yitshaq—or in English, Isaac—the name God gave to Abraham's son by Sarah, is normally translated *he laughs*. As I have indicated in *God's Poetry*, the shape of Isaac's life better fits the rhyming word 'esek', *dispute* or *contention*.

However, most significant of all—and the third hint within the text that God and Abraham are entering into a threshold covenant—is the Hebrew version of Isaac's name—Yitshaq—encodes a threshold-associated word. 'Shaq' has come down to us in Hebrew as *lintel* but, in Turkish, the closely-related word 'eşik', from Old Turkic 'isik', actually means *threshold*.

God's fondness for punning on 'shaq' cannot be doubted. It occurs in that interchange already mentioned with the prophet Jeremiah:

The word of the Lord came to me: 'What do you see, Jeremiah?'
'I see the branch of an almond tree,' I replied.
The Lord said to me: 'You have seen correctly for I am watching to see that my word is fulfilled.'

Jeremiah 1: 11–12 NIV

As previously indicated, this might seem completely irrelevant, even absurd. However, in Hebrew, it demonstrates God's sense of humour. He loves playing with words: 'shaqed', *almond,* is used here as a pun for 'shaqad', *watching*.

In addition, the connotation of the word 'shaqad', *watching,* is *to be wakeful*—and this is a lyrically appropriate description of the almond tree as it is traditionally the first to 'wake up' and bloom during the year.

Yes, the first to cross the threshold from winter to spring, to pass from one season to the next. Perhaps it's no coincidence that 'shaqed', *almond,* also contains the threshold-related element, 'shaq'.

Personally I think God, the poetic wordsmith, was using one of His favourite puns when He named Yitshaq. This name He gave to Abraham for his son not only echoes of laughter but also of the threshold covenant they happened to be undertaking at the very moment they were speaking and eating together. Indeed God and Abraham together demonstrated exactly how a threshold and salt covenant should be made.

Yet by the end of the same day, Abraham's nephew Lot had showed exactly the opposite: the devastating consequences when a threshold covenant goes seriously awry.

When an honoured guest takes his departure, as a mark of high regard his host walks with him out of town a distance the length of which is determined by the affectionate esteem in which the host holds his visitor ... So in ... the book of Genesis we are told that Abraham's guests 'rose up from thence, and looked toward Sodom: and Abraham went with them to bring them on the way.' The English phrase, however, 'to bring them on the way', *falls far short of expressing the full meaning of the term* 'shy-ya''.

Abraham Mitrie Rihbany, *The Syrian Christ*

When this book was still an unfinished manuscript, I badgered my mum into reading this chapter. Normally I dislike anyone seeing a raw draft, but I wanted new information on Toby and his nephew.

'I know this happened a long time ago,' I said to her. 'That's why I want you to read the story you told me, in the context I've placed it. I have a question to ask but, before I do, I want you to have a feel for what I'm really asking.'

'Right,' she said, once she'd finished. 'What's the question?'

'Let's assume, for the sake of argument, that Toby was an angel.'

'I'm not sure he was.'

'Nevertheless, if he was, then there has to have been a reason for him to turn up at that particular time. If we examine Scripture carefully, angels—especially pairs of them—are present at threshold moments. It's my view they are sent to guard spiritual doorways against the powers of constriction and wasting. And even if he wasn't an angel, I think he may have had a special sort of jurisdiction to ask for your protection as you approached a threshold. So, I want you to think back. What happened in the week after you met Toby?'

My mum has a prodigious memory. Still she thought for a very long time. Eventually she said, 'I can't be sure it was the week after. But it was definitely the same year. Your father mysteriously decided to come to church. It's hard to remember exactly when that happened but it can't have been long afterwards. Your dad suddenly gave up giving me a hard time about my faith and started exploring matters of spirituality.'

Threshold moment? Yes, that definitely qualified.

Angels often appear at great threshold moments in Scripture—heralds announcing the start of God's movement in a new and different way.

Think of the visit of the angel Gabriel to Mary to inform her she had been chosen as the mother of God's son. Or think of Zachary, the husband of Mary's cousin Elizabeth, struck dumb when he failed to believe Gabriel. Or the angel who announced Samson's birth to his parents. Or the angel who was neither for Joshua nor for his enemies.[42]

Or the two angels who told the disciples to stop looking up into the sky for Jesus but to get back to Jerusalem.

Yet they are not simply messengers: they are guardians of the threshold. From the many-eyed cherubim with their swords at the gateway of Eden, to the pair of angels who terrified the Roman soldiers guarding Jesus' tomb, they are the protectors of the time and place of change.

And if they're not there for you when you approach the threshold into your own destiny, you're in serious trouble. Because if they're not there, then the principalities and powers—the spirits of constriction and wasting, Python and its pals—are sure to be.

The cross is the only ladder high enough to touch heaven's threshold.

George Dana Boardman

The ancient importance of names and their significance as indicators of identity and destiny lasted well into the twentieth century in the Middle East. The modern state of Israel would almost certainly not exist but for the liberation of Jerusalem by ANZAC troops under British commander Allenby during the First World War.

What should have been a terrible siege was instead a comparatively easy victory. The Turkish defenders had orders from the Sultan of Constantinople to hold out at all costs. The ANZACs were, to all intents and purposes, headed into another Gallipoli—a battle impossible to win.

But the Turks of Jerusalem were uneasy. Allenby was now leading the allied troops: and they heard his surname as 'Allah nabi', *the prophet of Allah*.

It was unthinkable to oppose Allah or his prophet.

What should they do? Fight ... or surrender?

As they dithered, troubled in mind, the allied troops moved in.[43]

They took Jerusalem and headed up to Damascus, unaware the British and French had signed a pact, one which depended on who took the city. It was imperative to British foreign policy that Lawrence of Arabia in his armour-plated Rolls Royce, along with his Arab irregulars, enter Damascus first.

But they didn't. The ANZACs did. It was essential to keep that secret, to put a seal on it and keep it hidden from public knowledge. Medals were denied, field promotions refused, dispatches covered up.

The liberation of Damascus was the threshold moment in modern Middle Eastern history. It was Python's old territory. And it was waiting: almost a century later, Damascus is a perilous wasteland.

When a person—or a government—sacrifices others on a threshold, the spiritual ramifications are immense. Not just for those performing the sacrifice and those being sacrificed, but for the land itself. As the next story shows.

Ben Kish's father was a survivor of genocide. Along with some friends, he'd fled an attack on their little mountain village and had holed up for months in an isolated eyrie. When he was finally able to return home, he found his entire family had been wiped out, along with everyone else in his home town.

The life of Ben Kish's mother had also been shaped by abrupt violence. Ironically, her family had been massacred in retaliation for their failure to participate in that very same bout of ethnic cleansing that had annihilated his father's village. Only a few of the youngest girls in her village had survived. Trophies of war, they had been served up by the victors as a curious kind of 'guilt-ridden, belated apology' to men like her father.

Ben Kish consequently grew up in a whispering world of bitterness and hatred. Suppressed, destructive anger was apt to spring out of hiding at any moment. He was never sure whether the complex tangled loyalty his parents had for each other sprang from genuine love or from shared tragedy.

Both adored and indulged him. Nonetheless they were insanely fearful people. The world, they were sure, could change forever at any moment.

From the time he was a small boy, he heard his mother and her friends sigh about the terrible day their town was exterminated. His mother wasn't the only woman in the neighbourhood who'd been robbed of her childhood.

The laments of the women were quiet—almost secret—as if they were afraid. How he longed to comfort them—to do something, anything, to help. If only he'd been there that day when their village was attacked! In his childhood dreams, he saved the day and made his mother smile.

As Ben Kish grew older, he heard from his father the story behind the massacres. Black moods would overtake the boy as he thought about those monsters responsible. One day he would see they paid for their crimes.

In time, his father made good. Out of the ashes of the past, he created a new home in the village where he'd grown up. He did the best he could by his wife and prided himself on being a good provider. He built up a substantial livestock business.

But one day—just as his parents had been sure it would—the world changed in an instant. Ben Kish had grown into a tall, well-built young man with a quiet, modest air about him. His father entrusted him one day with finding some missing stock and, as he worked to fulfil this task, he crossed paths with a semi-government official. The man took an immediate shine to him.

Ben Kish, too, felt the almost instant rapport between them. The official happened to be on the lookout for someone to head up a newly formed government body. He was personally sure he'd found the perfect candidate and decided to offer him the appointment.

Ben Kish, despite being swept up in the thrill of it all, had his doubts. Then something happened to push them aside. His mother's village was attacked. It had been resettled and, although there was no one left there from his mother's day, that wasn't the point. All the dreams of his childhood rushed to the fore: although he couldn't save his mother long ago, he could save the people who now lived in his mother's village.

If only he had some official status, he was sure he could muster enough help to save the day.

The offer of the official seemed, in retrospect, to be almost miraculous in its timing. So he accepted.

Just in time! A jubilant population hailed him a hero. He'd rescued his mother's hometown from destruction and the people swore they'd never forget. To wild acclaim, he was confirmed in the government post he'd accepted.

All went well for a time—quite some years, as a matter of fact. He excelled in his position.

He was still subject to black, tormented thoughts from time to time—a legacy of the atmosphere he'd lived in as a child—but he'd been able to spare his son from its influence. The boy was everything a father could dream of and was loved by everyone.

Then one fine day, it all went pear-shaped. The grandson of one of the monsters responsible for the original massacre so long ago turned up. The kid was brave, talented and good-looking and, from the first, Ben Kish hated him. With a passion. When he heard the kid being praised, he was jealous too.

History—in the form of a genocidal massacre—was about to repeat itself.

All mankind is of one author and is one volume; when one man dies, one chapter is not torn out of the book, but translated into a different language ... any man's death diminishes me, because I am involved in mankind; and therefore never send to know for whom the bell tolls; it tolls for thee.

John Donne

I love the *Chronicles of Narnia* by CS Lewis. However, I disagree profoundly with one statement in them. Aslan tells Lucy in *Prince Caspian* that we can never know what 'might-have-been'. On the contrary, I think it's completely obvious, in certain instances, what some people are called to in life.

I hope you began to suspect the identity of Ben Kish by the end of the last section. Better known as Saul, son of Kish, he was the first king of Israel. His background was excessively harrowing—it is not an exaggeration to portray his father as a survivor of genocide and his mother a trophy of war.

I have taken a little liberty in suggesting heroic fantasies for his childhood. But probably not much.

It may not be totally accurate to say his father, Kish, fled the total obliteration of Gibeah. Possibly it was his grandfather, Abiel, instead.

Nevertheless, it is correct that, a generation or so back from Saul, there was major trauma. Mega-trauma. In both the male and female lines.

The modern science of epigenetics (epi: *upon*; epigenetics: *upon genes*) tells us that trauma can have a transient effect on genes which lasts for three or four generations. Saul was subject, not just to the sins of his fathers, but to the curses of a national calamity.

He wasn't being humble when he said he came from the smallest tribe in Israel: it was a simple fact. The people of Benjamin had been nearly wiped out by the other eleven tribes. A certain political expediency may therefore have been involved in his ratification as king: the Benjaminites could never lord it over the other tribes.[44]

Some serious curses descended Saul's family line—curses it was his calling in life to remove. As Samuel said on first meeting him, punning on his name, Saul and his family were the ones on whom all the '*desire*' of Israel focused.

The call on his life was to heal the land, reconcile the twelve tribes and stop the hatred about the massacres descending another generation. Saul almost—but not quite—succeeded. His conspicuous failure in his relationship with David allowed the past to repeat itself—not in broad brushstrokes but in fine, specific detail.

Genocide occurred again.

In violation of his covenant obligations, he committed atrocities against the Gibeonites.

The parallel between the two acts of genocide in different generations is completely clear: Gibeah and Gibeon even have the same meaning, *rocky hill*.

Long after Saul died, the consequences of his action still poisoned Israel. David, years later, desperately inquired of the Lord why prayer on behalf of the land wasn't being answered. He was informed that the reason went way back to Saul's destruction of the Gibeonites. In violating the covenant which, centuries previously, the people of Gibeon had cut with Joshua, Saul had unleashed all the curses entailed in breaking it.

It's all too easy to look at this example of a time when God did not answer prayer on behalf of the land and note, as many Christians today do, that David was left to contend with Saul's sin. This is a very simplistic view.

The long shadow of Saul's covenant violation at Gibeon goes back even before he was born. And it starts with a covenant violation in his hometown of Gibeah.

We know only that in some strange and melancholy way we have become a waste land.

Erich Maria Remarque, *All Quiet on the Western Front*

Some time before Saul was born, a priest lived in the hill country of Ephraim with his concubine. She left him and went home to her father in Bethlehem. After some months, the priest decided to go and woo her back. He succeeded and then, over a period of five days, enjoyed the congenial hospitality of his father-in-law.

Setting off late to return home with his concubine, he came to the town of Gibeah in the hill country of Benjamin. At nightfall, he waited for some time in the town square before finally being offered shelter. As is still common in the hospitality rites of the region, he came into covenant simply by passing over his host's threshold and breaking bread with him.

The men of Gibeah were a nasty lot. They conspicuously failed to offer this Levite hospitality and left him to linger in the town square. They then turned up at the home of his host and demanded he be sent out so they could have sexual relations with him.

The Levite's host was obligated by the threshold covenant to defend him—to the death, if necessary. He offered to give his own daughter to the men, just as Lot had once offered his virgin daughters to the men of Sodom to protect his visitors.

Instead, the concubine was thrown out to the men and gang-raped. After a night of abuse, she died trying to crawl back to the safety of the house. In her last moments, she made a gesture that would change the fortunes of Israel forever and directly impact the history of the nation for at least a century.

She put her hands on the threshold stone.

We've lost the significance and the drama of this gesture. She touched the sacred basin-like stone which caught any blood painted on the doorposts to let any guests know a calf, lamb or goat had been sacrificed in their honour and that the feast of welcome was ready.

Ultimately her symbolic action in touching this cornerstone, a stone always to be passed over, never stepped on, spoke louder than a thousand words of argument. Effectively she told her husband and his host that, while she should have been covered and defended by their threshold covenant, she had instead become its sacrificial victim.

The seriousness of upholding a threshold covenant can be seen in the story of Samson. The Philistines didn't dare attack Samson while he was protected by a threshold covenant, even if he happened to be carrying their town gates to ensure he remained within its safeguards.

So when the Levite sent his barbaric message to call the Israelites together to decide on a course of action, this understanding of the utter inviolability of a threshold covenant was in the background. The people of Gibeah had acted so dishonorably they were worse than the Philistines. They risked a judgment on Israel similar to the one following the most notorious threshold covenant violation in history: Sodom.

By the time the Israelites had gathered to attack Gibeah, the whole tribe of Benjamin had mustered to defend it. An isolated episode of violence had escalated into war. By the end, not only was Gibeah wiped out, almost the entire tribe of Benjamin had been killed. Only six hundred fighting men escaped to an oasis out in the desert.

In a belated attack of guilt, the other eleven tribes realised they'd gone too far. Way, way too far.

They'd meant to teach the people of Gibeah a lesson they'd never forget, not exterminate an entire tribe. With only six hundred men left and every woman dead, the Benjaminites could never get back on their feet.

Then, in a horrifying 'fix', the Israelites did a headcount and realised no one from Jabesh Gilead had answered their summons to war. So they decided that, to get wives for the Benjaminites, they'd kill everyone in Jabesh Gilead except for any unmarried young women. These girls were spared so they could be given to the six hundred out in the desert. Except there weren't quite enough women to go around. But that's another story.

Into this mind–blowing mess, Saul was born.

In each generation, God chooses individuals and calls them to heal national and familial wounds. It's no different now to how it was then. Chances are you are reading this book because it's your calling, too.

At the end of the period of the judges, the entire nation needed to reverse the curses of threshold covenant violation and the national rupture it had caused. Specifically:

- the twelve tribes needed to be reconciled with the people of Jabesh Gilead by extending protection to them in time of war
- the people of Gibeah needed to be reconciled with a priest of the hill country of Ephraim through a sustained friendship
- the people of Gibeah needed to be reconciled with the people of Bethlehem through the keeping of covenant

It may be surprising that Saul actually succeeded—superlatively—in carrying out two of these three tasks.

His first action after being anointed king was to save Jabesh Gilead—his mother's hometown. It was a heroic undertaking—the people of Jabesh Gilead didn't just say they were eternally grateful, they proved it. Decades later, they risked their lives to retrieve Saul's body from the Philistines after his death.

Samuel was the seer-priest who anointed Saul king. The opening verses of the book of Samuel tell us his background—his father is from the hill country of ... where else but Ephraim?

God had arranged Saul's life and the people in it so that the land might be healed and the tribes reconciled.

Yet by examining Saul's generational stream, we can recognise why he was so bitter, depressed and subject to tormented moods. Although I believe it's clear God's call on his life was to reconcile the tribes, he himself needed to have a singular quality to be able to achieve that: forgiveness.

Inevitably—because the problem had started with a covenant violation involving someone from Bethlehem—Saul was going to find himself in covenant relationship with someone from Bethlehem.

That someone was David.

David was Saul's armour-bearer, a position that meant they were blood brothers through the cutting of a covenant.

To reverse the curse coming down his generational stream, Saul had to keep covenant, not betray it.

Yet, by succumbing to jealousy and failing to forgive, he was never able to break free of the curse. He ignored his vows repeatedly, trying to kill David.

His son Jonathan[45] was the man Saul should have been: the covenant–keeper who brings blessing on the land, not perpetuates the cycle of harm.

We're called ... to oneness, not aloneness.

Anne Hamilton, *God's Panoply*

There's a tendency on the part of many preachers to rip Saul out of context and use him simply as a foil for David, the boy from Bethlehem. One is the man God rejected as king while the other was given His promise that his throne would last forever.

Anyone who is not vastly troubled by this surely needs to examine the case more closely.

Saul was an excellent father. Jonathan himself is evidence of this. Moreover Jonathan, until David came on the scene, had no reason to consider his father duplicitous. There is no record of Saul being faithless to his wife or setting a man up to go to his death simply so he could enjoy illicit sexual favours, as David notably did in the case of Bathsheba and Uriah. True, Saul may have wanted to kill David but then David wanted to kill both Joab and Shimei. While keeping his promise not to harm them, David nonetheless left instructions that, once he was dead, for Solomon to ensure they were executed.

Furthermore, in contrast with Saul, David was an appalling father. His inaction over Amnon's rape of Tamar and further inaction when Absalom flees to his maternal grandfather Talmai (note the threshold–related name!) set the kingdom up for major disaster.

Yet David was a man 'after God's own heart'.

Saul's sin came to affect the land itself. Why didn't David's? Why did God favour David and not Saul? What was the difference?

It's all about covenant. God is a covenant-keeper par excellence. David, for all his many and varied faults, was also a covenant-keeper.

True, David was descended from a line of covenant-keepers—starting with that threshold covenant of Rahab—and Saul came from exactly the opposite. His ancestors broke covenant and, although he made great inroads into overcoming that generational issue, ultimately he failed. In doing so, he broke his own personal covenant with David. He broke the divine covenant by disobeying the Law and offering a sacrifice which only a priest should tender to God. He broke the tribal covenant between the Israelites and the Gibeonites.

In the last case, his repetition of the sins of his forefathers resulted in a curse over the land which was not lifted until many years after his death. If David ever broke covenant, surely it was when he handed the family of Saul—whom he was obligated to protect—over to the Gibeonites.

Psalm 7 is prefaced with: *'A shiggaion of David, which he sang to the Lord concerning Cush, a Benjamite.'*

Shiggaion is an unusual word, often suggested as an instruction to the musician. However, it is related to words for *to misjudge* or *make a mistake*. As Jewish scholars point out, there is no other mention of someone named Cush from the tribe of Benjamin in Scripture. It is almost certainly a reference to Saul—but in what context?

Rabbi Yechiel Eckstein says: 'The Sages offer two possibilities. The first is when David sang a song of praise to God after Saul was finally killed at the hands of the Philistines.' It was inappropriate to celebrate the death of an anointed king. The second possibility, according to Eckstein, is when David cut off a piece of Saul's robe. Saul didn't know David was hiding in the cave and could have killed him, as his men were urging. Instead David spared his life but took a piece of his cloak in order to prove his good intentions. Eckstein points out: 'Again … his actions were still wrong because he had lifted a hand against God's appointed king of Israel.'

This may be so, though David's comment to his men seems to indicate, in my view, he *refused* to lift his hand against the Lord's anointed.

I believe there's a third possibility: David had made a terrible mistake in not keeping his covenant obligations to the family of Saul. He knew it … far too late. His deep regret in handing them over to the Gibeonites and his plea for God's forgiveness could well be recorded in Psalm 7.

Breaking one covenant to bring an end to the devastating consequences of another broken covenant? Not smart. The cycle could easily have started again, but for God's mercy and David's contrite heart.

In the twenty-first century, here's a lesson we need to learn. To bring a contrite heart before God for:

- keeping covenants we should have cut off (generations ago)—covenants with death, darkness, principalities, powers and world rulers, *or*
- failing to keep covenants we should have—those with our Father in heaven, with Jesus of Nazareth and with the Holy Spirit, *or*
- both of the possibilities above

I would be true, for there are those who trust me;
I would be pure, for there are those who care;
I would be strong, for there is much to suffer;
I would be brave, for there is much to dare.
I would be friend of all—the foe, the friendless;
I would be giving, and forget the gift.
I would be humble, for I know my weakness;
I would look up— and laugh— and love— and lift.

Howard Arnold Walter

There's a mysterious connection between names and threshold covenants which occurs throughout Scripture. The importance of names when it comes to destiny is often overlooked in the modern world. Even when we do recognise their value, we tend to overrate the dictionary definition and underrate the poetry.

Ever since I realised no linguist has ever successfully explained how James came to be derived from Jacob—and occasionally an expert will admit to this—I've had misgivings about its assigned meaning of *supplanter*. When, in addition, I realised every James of my acquaintance acts just like Jamin, the perfect *right hand* man, and not like Jacob, the *usurper*, I decided dictionaries have immense limitations.

More importantly, while they are sometimes a great starting point, I've come to believe it is actually immaterial whether they are right or wrong.

What people believe in their own hearts about their names is far more significant. An individual's instinctive understanding of the derivation of a name is always closer to the true meaning than any other definition. It's the power plug whose power source is with God.

The way John's gospel records the story of 'doubting Thomas', not long after Peter's denial, might lead us to suspect 'the disciple Jesus loved' was building himself a pedestal as high as my dad's. Maybe there was still a vestige of wanting to be one of those seated on Jesus' right and left hand when He came into His kingdom.

However, as I said before, I believe he chose to tell Thomas' story because it revealed the final undoing of a long-standing curse over the tribes of Israel. He wanted to record for the Jewish people the overcoming of a threshold 'seal' when doubt is replaced by faith.

My mum was mostly, but not entirely, convinced destiny is encoded in names and that poetry is as significant as meaning. It was Alison's story that finally tipped her over the edge. Who would have thought a rhyming name like Taliesin was the key? My mum had never even heard of Taliesin. But here she was an active participant in a case that defied her doubts about Scriptural names being given *after* a defining event and not *before*.

She had known Alison for more than twenty years and, in fact, had counselled her several times. She thought she knew her extremely well but she'd never, even for a moment, guessed at the stunning level of musical talent Alison had.

My mum was also aware that, had I not started asking questions to ascertain the level of parallelism of Alison with Taliesin, not a shred of evidence about any musical ability would ever have come to light. Together we quizzed her about what she sensed God had told her over the years.

Long ago, it seemed, He'd definitively answered prayers regarding her songs ... but He'd been silent for quite some time. He hadn't answered any questions about destiny or identity for ages.

All there had been, that she was aware of, was a vision about some pink roses once when someone had prayed for her.

It's always tricky to know what God means by roses: in my view, it's different depending on whether it's a picture or a word.

Pictures, I tend to think, are references to the ancient concept of 'sub rosa': the rose painted on the ceiling that adjures those present 'under the rose' to keep everything said in that place secret.

Words, on the other hand, are more likely to be translations—or rather mistranslations—of the Hebrew word Ha'bazlith, the name which the Shulamite—Solomon's bride—gives to herself. Although Ha'bazlith Sharon is translated as *rose of Sharon*, it is almost certainly not a rose but a daffodil-like plant with a yellow trumpet and creamy petals: the narcissus tazetta.

Shakespeare famously told us that a rose by any other name would smell as sweet, suggesting thereby that names are irrelevant.

Yet the narcissus tazetta has profoundly different senses in different languages. From the Greek legend of Narcissus, after whom the flower draws its botanical name, we get the word narcissism: self-centred, self-absorbed self-obsession. Scott Peck in his remarkable book *People of the Lie* suggests narcissism is strongly linked to evil. (Yes, narcissism! The very thing that has become a virtue in the age of YouTube and Facebook.)

Ha'bazlith Sharon, on the other hand, is the Hebrew name for the same fragrant flower. It proclaims a sense so different to narcissism, it's almost a polar opposite. In fact, Ha'bazlith Sharon may well be one of the most remarkable phrases in all Scripture. Paul, I believe, was thinking of it when he instructed, 'Put on the breastplate of righteousness.'

Sharon is related to shiryan, *body armour—a coat of mail* or a *breastplate*. It is derived from 'yashar', *make straight, be level, be lawful, be just*. How neat and tidy is this? A single word, 'sharon', sums up Paul's image: the breastplate of righteousness.

Books on the meanings of names tend to write off the popular girl's name Sharon as *the plain* but there's so much more to it than that.

The poetry God writes within names about our identity and destiny works on several principles. The fourth one of these discussed in *God's Poetry* is the associative principle. When one word is consistently associated with another, then it's possible for the destiny of one to be shaped by the meaning of the other. For instance: Jericho was traditionally part of the phrase 'Jordan of Jericho'. Jericho does not mean *fall down* but Jordan does.

Thus Sharon, in being consistently coupled with Ha'bazlith, has acquired some other extraordinary overtones.

God intends for each and every Sharon of this world to be a warrior maid decked out in a jewelled breastplate of righteousness. That might be enough to go on with, but she has even more surprises up her sleeve. Or is it gauntlet?

Names, after all, are prophetic poetry. It's not just about the meaning, it's about the song.

Solomon's betrothed, 'the Rose', goes by the name Ha'bazlith. This has, according to Arie Uittenbogaard, several layered senses. The first of which is 'she has peels' or 'she has many layers'. Altogether appropriate for a flower springing up from an onion-like bulb.

So Ha'bazlith Sharon tells us—obliquely, through her name—that she has many coats of armour. And lest with the appellation 'Sharon' we think of a warrior princess bride kitted out in a flak jacket, it's worth examining the deeper meaning of the word for *rose*: 'bazlith', also spelt 'havatzelet' or 'chabatstseleth'.[46]

Arie Uittenbogaard suggests 'chabatstseleth' is put together in such a way that its meaning is actually *overshadowed by God's love*.[47]

This perfectly fits the very unusual Hebrew thought which equates '*to put on armour*' with '*to kiss*'.[48] We are armoured against daily onslaughts by God's love—or, at least, we should be. That's His defence strategy for us. Sometimes we're reluctant to take this strategy on board. Sometimes we're huffy about life and we don't want to lift our faces for His kiss, and thereby receive His divine armour.

This sense of a reconciling kiss as the equivalent of putting on battle gear is embedded in Paul's description of the Armour of God. As I've pointed out in *God's Panoply*, up until at least the time of the Middle Ages it was obvious to Christians the kiss was there. However, it's not so obvious to us. Equally, it isn't obvious the daffodil-like 'chabatstseleth' is one of a total of seven flowers alluded to in the passage, either.

But perhaps it should have been: the 'chabatstseleth', after all, has many onion-like layers.

The meaning of names cannot be encapsulated in one or two words. The prophetic poetry of Sharon, for instance, is more than *a plain*—it's also *righteousness, breastplate, song, rose* and *overshadowed by God's love*—and that's just for starters!

And all names are like this!

Magnificent, strange and deep carriers of what we are called to be.

3

Woven Stone

CS LEWIS IS ONE of my favourite authors. One of his books that has risen steadily in my estimation over the years is the children's fantasy, *The Silver Chair*.

It's almost a manual on the tricks and tactics of Python. Indeed the Lady who lures Prince Rilian from the fountain assumes the form of a monstrous snake at the climax of the story and tries to crush him to death. The heroes find their way underground to rescue Prince Rilian through a giant letter E, suggesting that the Lady was meant to evoke an image of the 'Pythoness' of Delphi, an oracular shrine famed for its navelstone carved with a mysterious E.

I believe a large part of the enduring popularity of Lewis' seven–book series *The Chronicles of Narnia* is that they offer spiritual insight into problems we don't even know we have. Most of us don't know about Python, let alone how it operates. Yet the story offers us clues:

- there's a repeated attack on memory, made easier by a failure to be diligent in guarding it
- when we do remember, we soon forget
- our faith is weakened through a failure to strengthen our memories
- the giants who guard the threshold are out to make a meal of us
- we are assailed by thoughts of, 'If only ...'
- Python wants to steal our destiny so it can use its power to achieve its own purposes

- the more we fight it in our own strength, the more Python seeks to crush us
- we can put ourselves in Python's hands through our own folly
- Python prefers to mislead through ambiguous information rather than outright lies
- Python can be found cheerfully traversing the wasteland; it's got friends there who are experts in wasting
- the spirit of silence is one of Python's allies

The really interesting aspect of the novel is that it starts with an evocation of a very particular name covenant. The massive fall of Jill into Narnia at the beginning of the story which ends with a watery splash should remind us of the nursery rhyme, *Jack and Jill*, and of Lewis' own nickname: Jack.

This is about as coincidental as the fact that Lewis is derived from *llew*, the Welsh word for *lion*.

Once you start to poke around with names and the covenants surrounding them, you quickly begin to realise the need to be suited up in a full suit of armour. Just in case there's the spiritual equivalent of a landmine under the surface where you're digging.

When I was a teenager, I developed a quirky habit. If I was distressed, I'd jump up and whirl around on the spot until I felt better. I have no idea what inspired me to start in the first place. Other kids might have smoked, done drugs or looked for love in all the wrong places, but I just twirled on the spot. At some stage in my twenties, I stopped—mainly because there wasn't enough room in the house where I was boarding. And then I proceeded to forget about it.

It all sounds so incredibly innocent, doesn't it? It doesn't look like the spiritual equivalent of an unexploded bomb, does it? The deadliest sins are often the ones that seem most innocuous—the ones so apparently harmless you don't recognise them for what they are and you'd likely laugh if anyone suggested they were a deliberate insult directed against God's holiness.

Having worked with many people over long periods regarding

covenants, there are three elements I consider absolutely critical prior to making a start:

First, *prayer to restore belief in a happy ending*. It's startling how many Christians do not believe in their heart of hearts that 'happily ever after' is actually possible.

Secondly, *prayer to restore memory*. The most efficient weapon in Satan's arsenal, to my mind, is 'forgetting'. If you've forgotten your sins—or even your quirky, apparently harmless habits—you can't repent of them. You can be reaping the whirlwind and have no idea why, because your memory of what you've sown is gone.

Thirdly, *prayer to remove the need for haste*.

'*Those who believe will not be in haste*' is the inscription on the cornerstone of redemption recorded in Isaiah 28:16 KJV.

To cross the threshold into our destiny, our spiritual armour needs to be in tip–top shape. We need protection from Python and Rachab, the spirits of constriction and wasting lurking on the threshold.

There are several other issues we face besides these particular guardians but let's look at those matters later. Assuming we get past the threshold guards, we're not out of danger yet. Remember the three sons of Anak? Yes, there's a third spirit we have to face: the one whose job it is to whip us back across the threshold, bleeding and wounded and so disheartened we'll never try to come into our destiny again. This is Leviathan, the spirit of backlash, the king of the 'sons of pride'.

Leviathan is described as a twisty serpent and, for me, it's a delight to know it has turned up. It's a moment to pause and praise God. The threshold has been crossed! Things are going so well the enemy has called up reinforcements.

My delight springs from more than that, however. Before ever I heard of Leviathan as the spirit of backlash, before ever I realised it was a name associated with the rule of parliament instead of that of a king, I'd often encountered it in one of my favourite passages of the Bible: God's reply to Job.

God's delight in Leviathan in Psalm 124 as it dances and frolics is evident. His enthusiasm splashes over the page. Until I started to hear differently, I always thought Leviathan was the clown of God's creation. Dangerous, certainly, but also graceful and majestic.

And I haven't changed my mind.

God's judgment on all of His own creation was that it was good.

That clearly and explicitly includes Leviathan.

It clearly and implicitly includes Python and Rachab.

It is very important to stress here a point John Paul Jackson makes in his thoughtful and highly recommended book, *Needless Casualties of War*. All of God's creation, even the fallen parts of it, should be accorded the utmost respect and honour. To revile and curse celestial dignitaries is to set ourselves in judgment of God's creation and ultimately of God Himself. Moreover it's in direct violation of the Scriptural injunction in Jude 1:8–10 which also indicates that to make a slanderous accusation against an angelic entity invites destructive retaliation.

Keep your focus on God.

Honour everyone.

It's worth repeating: keep your focus on *God*, not angels. And honour everyone.

Python and Rachab were, in my view, once cherubim—and they still fulfill that same role of guarding a threshold while serving a different master. Leviathan, from its description, seems to have once been a seraph—one of the guardians of God's throneroom, an exalted angelic officer whose name means *shining burning* or *fire serpent*.

Their high rank has not been stripped from them. The gifts and calling of God are irrevocable.[49]

Therefore, put your armour on and honour everyone.

It is appropriate to apologise to God for dishonouring His creation, if you have hurled abuse at principalities and powers. Or even, on a different level, at government officials. It's a matter for repentance and reconciliation.

We are to honour the rank, regardless. Just as we should honour the Presidency, regardless of our political persuasion or the occupant of the office, so we should honour the position God has given His angelic guardians.

Paul modelled just how quickly we should back off. He had been brought before the Council and hit on the mouth by order of Ananias. Turning on Ananias, unaware he was the high priest, Paul spat out an accusation of hypocrisy:

'God is about to strike you, you whitewashed wall! Do you sit as a judge to try me in accordance with the Law, and yet in defiance of the Law you order me to be struck?'

Acts 23:3 AMP

The moment he was informed he had insulted the high priest, he backed down and admitted his fault. He recognised a violation of the Scriptural injunction in Exodus 22:28 which tells us not to speak ill of our rulers. Similarly Jude 1:8–10 tells us not to speak ill of any member of the angel hosts, even fallen ones.

Now the following is my personal opinion: to the degree we have dishonoured others—this includes other people, government bodies and leaders, various institutions, church denominations and so on—then to that same degree, Leviathan can injure us. To the level we have discourteously separated truth from love in dealing with others, then to that same degree, the guardians of honour can reproach us.

I repeat: keep your focus on God, put on your armour and honour everyone.

The Israelites were trapped. Pharoah with his chariots was coming up fast behind; in front of them was the Sea. God gave Moses very specific instructions:

'Tell the sons of Israel to turn back and camp before Pi–hahiroth, between Migdol and the sea; you shall camp in front of Baal–zephon, opposite it, by the sea.'

Exodus 14:1 NAS

Most people, unless they're seriously into geography, tend to read straight over this. But there's more than geography here.

The Romans of a much later era were aware of a concept we've lost: genius loci, *the spirit of a place*. The cliffs of Pi–hahiroth were not simply sheer rock faces. Migdol was not simply a watchtower for the Egyptian army, nor was Baal–zephon just a fortified border post.

The meaning of the names is instructive:

- Pi–hahiroth: Strong's lexicon says *place where sedge grows* and Cornwall & Smith suggests *mouth of wrath* or *kindlings*
- Migdol: *tower, guard tower* or *watchtower*
- Baal–zephon: *lord of the north*

Zaphon, *north*, has puzzled me for years. While it's fairly rare in Scripture, its poetic and prophetic patterning turns up in unexpected places—indicating covenantal overtones.[50] Yet its wider sense has always been elusive; still I felt a significant clue was this placename, Baal–zephon, *the lord of the north*, which is mentioned twice in Exodus.

Only when I discovered Erik Langkjer's analysis of the name 'Python' did this make sense. Langkjer relates Python to Typhon—an ancient Canaanite chaos–bringer which is the origin of our modern word *typhoon*. He derives Typhon in turn from Zaphon, *north*.

Now the Hebrew word for *south* is identical to *sea*.

So, when the Israelites faced Baal–zephon by the sea, they were confronting two spirits who claim dominion of the North and the South.

'You rule the raging of the sea; when its waves arise, You still them. You have broken Rachab in pieces, with Your mighty arm, You have scattered Your enemies.'

Psalm 89:9–10 AMP

Now Job 9:13 identifies Rachab as a sea monster and Isaiah 51:9–10 is suggestive of a spirit dwelling in the sea. However, it is equally clear from Isaiah 30:7 that Rachab is a name for Egypt. I therefore understand Rachab to be the name of a principality—the power behind the Pharaohs—and also a monstrous spirit whose natural domain is the sea.

Rachab and Python[51] seem to be mentioned together in Job 26:12–13. As spirits who claim ownership of the South and North—not to mention everything in between—they make a formidable foe. By creating the perfect typhoon-like storm in your life, they want to cause you such heartache through the constriction and wasting you experience, you'll go back with relief into slavery and never approach the threshold of freedom again.

And if this doesn't work, you'll have to contend with the spirit behind Pi-hahiroth.

Commonly, whenever I've worked with people regarding their threshold issues, one of the first signs of the defeat of Rachab and Python is the appearance of Leviathan.

Bearing in mind Cornwall & Smith's translation of Pi-hahiroth as *mouth of wrath* or *kindlings*, note this description of Leviathan from Job 41:19–21 NAS: *'Out of his mouth go burning torches; sparks of fire leap forth ... His breath kindles coals, and a flame goes forth from his mouth.'*

Pi-hahiroth is, I believe, mentioned to indicate the overwhelming nature of the spiritual enemies ranged against the Israelites:

- Python, the spirit of constriction
- Rachab, the spirit of wasting
- Leviathan, the spirit of backlash

And let's not forget Migdol, the watchtower.

Remember God's pun to Jeremiah about watching and almonds? The pun may well be multi-lingual. The amygdala, named from the Latin for *almond*, an almond-shaped group of nuclei in the brain, is like a tiny watchtower. Every second, it processes thousands of sense impressions bombarding us, filtering aside the ordinary and alerting us to potential danger. Here is the repository of 'fear memory'—when we encounter similar circumstances that, in the past, have led to traumatic incidents, we are forewarned by the amygdala that danger approaches.

Thresholds are often traumatic places for those of us who have encountered Python or Rachab previously. Fear memory can be so strong that, as a new doorway into destiny opens up, we pull back from it and sabotage our own chances.

The watchtower on the threshold is meant to help, not hinder. It is like the mezuzah observant modern Jews affix to a doorway. Often referred to as a watch over the door, the mezuzah contains a scroll, fulfilling the command of the Lord in Deuteronomy 6:9 to remember the Lord's commands by writing them on the doorposts and gates of each house.

While the mezuzah is about memory, the migdol that produces fear results in forgetfulness. And here is Satan's most cunning strategy.

Are you worried about your memory?

Consider the possibility you are under attack by the enemy's most deadly, efficient and successful agent. The true quiet achiever of demonic destruction is none other than the spirit of forgetfulness.

How can you repent of sin if you don't remember it?

How can you reconcile with friends or family when you've forgotten your hateful behaviour?

I'm not talking about repressed or suppressed memories: I'm talking about a spirit which raids our thoughts so short-term memory is never processed long-term. (Such processing is another function of the amygdala when it's operating properly.)

We simply forget.

We start to worry about our memory.

The Israelites themselves found this spirit hardest to deal with. They so quickly forgot the miracles the Lord had performed in rescuing them from Egypt. They forgot His provision and protection.

If it's occurred to you this spirit is a problem in your life, take a moment right now to ask for God's help. Don't leave it until later because you'll almost certainly forget.

Father God, I ask You to put Your own guard on my amygdala and memory and to dismiss any guard not sent by You. Please help me to remember from now on and also to seal those new memories by the power of Your Holy Spirit. Please also bring to mind anything from the past You desire me to deal with and remind me to seek the immediate help of Your son, Jesus of Nazareth. Help me also to remember to pray regularly about the restoration of my memory. I ask this in the name of my covenant redeemer, Jesus of Nazareth, who died for me.

It's my experience that, over time, such a prayer makes a distinct, encouraging difference for many people who have never before considered the possibility their failing memory is a spiritual, rather than physical, problem.

You may be thinking: why should I have to contend with any of these principalities, powers or spirits? It doesn't make sense to me. Didn't Jesus triumph over every single one of them?

Isn't it all done at the Cross?

Again, what 'all' does this question refer to? If it's the 'all' of salvation, *yes*, it's true we can add absolutely nothing to what Jesus accomplished through His death. Salvation is by the grace of God.

Nothing else.

Yet it's also true we are saved by faith. So we need to be careful this question doesn't reduce our thinking to a trivial, simplistic level. It's all too easy to extol a post-modern understanding of what it means to be a Christian: faith without fidelity, reconciliation without repentance, grace without gratitude, restoration without relationship, covenant without conditions, worship without work,[52] trust without truth.

Any definition of 'salvation by faith' that comes closer to meaning *assent to right doctrinal values* rather than *full-on covenantal friendship with, and uplift of, Jesus* has a staggering blindspot.

If we believe that, because all our sins are already automatically dealt with at the Cross then we don't need to worry about repenting of specific issues, we've misunderstood the nature of faith.

We are not saved by faithfulness, we're saved by faith. Yet we also need to divest ourselves of any mindset seeking to divorce faithfulness from faith.

Despite all the spiritual opposition the Israelites had to deal with, they escaped Pharaoh's armies and made it across the Red Sea to freedom. At their head was the pillar of cloud by day and fire by night, along with the angel of the Lord. Yes, as they crossed the threshold, the cherubim guarded them.

Python and Rachab, the dark spirits of the north and the south, have fallen from the role God appointed them to undertake—instead of guarding our passage across thresholds, they seek to squeeze and squander us.

The most common way is financial, but that's not their only trick.

A literary agent had negotiated a stunning deal for a new client. She'd sold a book for a six-figure advance and was excited about the author working with the editorial team who were all enthusiastic about the project. Then, one by one, the staff who had been most passionate about the book left to go into business for themselves or were headhunted to work for other companies.

By the time the book was ready to go to press, no one was left who had championed it in the first place—and those who replaced them had absolutely no interest in it. In fact, they couldn't understand why a no-name author had been given such an extraordinary advance. With no staff to rev up the marketing department into a high-level promotion, the book bombed. And with a disastrous track record, it's been almost impossible for that author to interest a publisher in any other work.

In this case the constriction is not money—just the opposite. It's about an inability to get a message into the market.

When we are approaching a threshold, it's wise to talk to God about two issues:

- ask Him to help you remember if you have ever insulted a celestial being, good or bad. If 'yes', tell Him you repent for failing to heed Jude 1:9 and ask for His forgiveness for lack of respect towards His creation and Him as a creator.
- ask Him whether it's time for the cherubim to guard the threshold you are approaching. If He says 'no', it could be you're not ready or else the threshold is a false one. If He says 'yes', then ask for His mercy and grace to flow to you as you ask for this new watch over your threshold. Because without that mercy and grace, you're putting yourself in great danger.

The cherubim are holy: they guard the mercy-seat of God on the Ark of the Covenant. When Uzzah touched the Ark to stop it from falling, he dropped dead. He clearly had the best of intentions but his action was still lacking in caution.[53]

Just as Aslan in *The Lion, the Witch and the Wardrobe* is not a tame lion, so the cherubim are not without their perilous aspect. They are warrior guardians of thresholds and they can deal with Python and Rachab without our help. However, if we rashly get in the way, we need to understand the consequences may be extreme.

Our jobs are to let the cherubim do their job, as well as keep our eyes on God and to hold His hand as He leads us. And because God inhabits the praises of His people, the best way to keep hold of Him is through praise.

There are lots of traps and tricks—quite apart from any dark spirits—which are designed as failsafes to stop us crossing into our destiny. To avoid them, we need to listen to the still, small voice of the Holy Spirit.

We're going to face more opposition: Python and Rachab may call up their friends. The Israelites, having crossed the Red Sea, got so scared they couldn't take the last step out of the passage between the thresholds: on spotting the sons of Anak, *the choker*, they forgot everything God had done. They forgot that God was fighting for them and thought they had to do it all alone.

The fact is that, even when we've got past the threshold, Python wants to make a comeback and, unless you've got a Joshua or Caleb mentality, it's going to succeed.

So: remember to remember. Remember the acts of God on your behalf and, if you've had memory problems, remember to pray about remembering the acts of God on your behalf.

Because the last of the principalities we have to face on crossing a threshold is the one that wants to whip us right back across it and slam us so hard we never recover. The spirit of backlash has arrived, that most fearsome of God's created wonders: Leviathan.

Both Levi and Leviathan come from the same root, *to join* or *to adhere*. It seems odd at first that the twisting fleeing dragon—as Leviathan is described by Isaiah—can be in any way connected with the Levites, God's chosen and appointed priests.

Names, as I repeatedly pointed out in *God's Poetry*, all encode a choice. 'Destiny' is what God has called us to but we can refuse our calling. Or miss out on it, due to any number of factors. We're not fated to achieve it.

Haimona, Alison and Rick all show the complexity of circumstances bearing on the matter.

Levi and Leviathan are two names which show us the ups and downs of name covenants and the in-built choices they offer. A notable and similar example in *God's Poetry* is that of Korah.

All names are ultimately given by God. All names are governed by covenants which are ultimately ours to choose or refuse. There is no name so negative it cannot be redeemed; no name so positive it cannot be corrupted; no name about which we can assume unadulterated holiness for ourselves or any member of our family; no name where we can sit back in relief and decide nothing needs to be done.

When Levi's father, Jacob, blessed his twelve sons at the end of his life, most of his attention was given to Judah and Joseph. The double portion Reuben should have received as the firstborn effectively was split between Joseph's two sons. Levi hardly got a mention—in fact, while it's perfectly obvious a future king would arise from the tribe of Judah, there's nothing to suggest Levi's descendants would form a priesthood. Jacob instead prophesies the Levites will be scattered and divided amongst the tribes of Israel—contrary to the meaning of the name.

Yet God's plan to prosper them was always there. Their calling was to unite the tribes—'join', as their name suggests—though often they did the opposite. So where does the calling to be priests originate?

Personally I think it's hidden in the relationship of Levi's name to the twisting, fleeing, armour-plated ruler of the sons of pride, Leviathan. As previously noted, I suspect Leviathan is one of the six-winged, burning, serpent-like seraphim, albeit a fallen one. An additional reason for suspecting this is the similarity of Levi's calling to the function of a seraph.

Just as the seraphim are uniquely present in the throneroom of God, so too the Levites have an exclusive calling in the presence of God.[54] Alone amongst the Israelites, the high priest could approach God's throne within the veil of the Temple on the Day of Atonement.

Just as the seraphim are the guardians of the throneroom of God, the Levites were the guardians of the inner court of the Temple. Only the high priest's armour enabled him to safely enter the Holy of Holies—and that armour was the blood of the sacrifice.

And I said to the man who stood at the gate of the year: 'Give me a light that I may tread safely into the unknown.'

And he replied: 'Go out into the darkness and put your hand into the Hand of God. That shall be to you better than light and safer than a known way.'

Minnie Louise Haskins

It should be easy to subdue threshold guardians like Python, Rachab and Leviathan. The staff Moses threw before Pharoah and which turned into a snake shows his mastery of Leviathan. Perhaps when Jesus said His followers would be able to trample on snakes and scorpions without harm, spiritually He meant Leviathan.

We should also be able to best Leviathan's servants, the 'sons of pride'. Now since Rachab means *arrogance*, it's probable it should be counted amongst this select band. It's difficult to determine how many 'sons of pride' there are but I've encountered a few. The most significant for me personally is *silence*.[55]

So why do we come off second best so often in these encounters? I believe it's because we retain covenants with the very cosmic spirits we are asking to allow us to pass. I believe that the very mysterious episode when Moses leaves for Egypt and God tries to kill him on the way indicates the immensely serious nature of trying to step into a call from God while our covenantal relationship with Him is amiss. From the text it's unclear whether Moses undertook a threshold covenant he should not have or whether he failed to keep covenant obligations for his son. What is clear is that Zipporah, Moses' wife, realised the issue was to do with covenant violation and took action.

Like Zipporah, we need to take decisive steps about the way we've ignored God's covenant. We've got to stop thinking of covenant as contract—as having more to do with law than grace. The essential nature of covenant is oneness with another.

And we can't be one with God while we're one with His enemies.

Perversely, we want Python and Rachab to extend grace to us by breaking their own covenant with us to their own disadvantage! We might protest we didn't agree to any covenant. Whether those covenants were taken out by us or our ancestors doesn't matter: they are still legally binding.

Grace and mercy are attributes solely of God, so if we're expecting this as we approach a threshold where Python and friends hold sway, we're a bit confused about who God is.

We're even more confused about the covenantal nature of the threshold. Now when it comes to dealing with ungodly covenants of previous generations, I'm a huge advocate of the Scriptural injunction: '*Those who believe will not be in haste.*'

There are traps and mazes to avoid and they are customised for each of us individually. Thresholds are complex, dangerous places protected by a threefold guard:

- the watch
- the stone
- the seals

That threefold guard should remind us of the tomb of Jesus. The resurrection was in fact the crossing of the ultimate threshold: that from death to life. Yet crossing any spiritual threshold has similarities to a 'resurrection problem'.

Consider: after Jesus was raised from the dead, He still had to get out of the tomb. He had to overcome the three problems mentioned in Matthew 27:66—namely, the watch (the Roman guards), the stone (in front of the tomb) and the seal (the governor's surety to deter grave robbers).

If we cast our minds back to the passage of the Israelites through the Red Sea, we can see the parallel: the Roman watch is like the triplet of Pi-hahiroth, Baal-zephon, and the sea—hence the soldiers are like the three cosmic powers who guard thresholds. The stone and the seal are harder to spot in the story of the Exodus. However, I find it utterly fascinating there is a 'Migdol', a guardian of memory, present in the story of the resurrection. God lets us know her role through her name. Magdala is actually from migdol, *watchtower*.

Without Mary Magdalen, would many of the details surrounding the resurrection be known? I doubt it.

Let's examine yet another threshold situation: the crossing of the Jordan by the Israelites under the command of Joshua. Thirty–eight years previously the Israelites had turned back, frightened by the likes of Talmai, Ahiman and Sheshai, the gigantic sons of Anak. But this time, the Israelites have faith and are thus afforded angelic protection. The Commander of the Armies of the Lord appears and frightens Joshua. This is Joshua the unfrightenable, remember? The one who thought Talmai, Ahiman and Sheshai weren't such a big deal.

Prior to this, while they are going from Shittim to Gilgal—'*passing over*' is the term used, just in case, I guess, later readers should miss the threshold overtones of the event—they pick up twelve stones from the dry bed of the Jordan to serve as a memorial. The stones parallel both the Migdol of the Exodus and the Magdalen of Jesus' resurrection. They also double as a parallel for the stone blocking the doorway of the tomb.

The Israelites, by the time they were about to cross the Jordan, had figured out something we generally miss: it's a bad idea to have covenantal relations with anyone other than Yahweh. A very bad idea.

So they ratify their covenant with Him right after they pass over the Jordan. This is a point at which they really needed the cherubim to protect them because, after being circumcised, they weren't exactly in peak fighting mode.[56]

Thresholds have many common spiritual elements. Although we've examined many cases—some where the keeping of covenant brought blessing and others where a violation brought disaster—the overall patterns may not be obvious. So let's summarise them.

	Godly Covenant	Ungodly Covenant
Stone	is passed over	is trampled on
Twin guard	cherubim, perilous and holy	Python and Rachab, the constrictor and waster
Extra guard	seraphim: officers who maintain honour	Leviathan: spirit of backlash
Watchtower & memory	is renewed through prayer and focus on God; symbolised by the mezuzah	is scattered and taken by defiling spirits; symbolised by any protective 'ward'.
Engraving on stone	an explicit or implied "If..." statement connected to love or faith.	an explicit or implied "If..." statement connected to death
Seal	the word of God and the indwelling of the Holy Spirit	a curse or dedication to a spirit designed as an explosive failsafe
Sacrifice	praise for the all-sufficient sacrifice of Jesus	self or others
Armour	on	off
Key	is available and enables a proper exercise of authority within a given jurisdiction	has been stolen, allowing spirits to deny authority and due jurisdiction
Inheritance or destiny	restored	lost
Long term effect	blessing continues over inheritance for several generations	social disruption on a major scale until even the land itself needs healing

Love's redeeming work is done;
Fought the fight, the battle won;
Vain the stone, the watch, the seal;
Christ has burst the gates of hell.

Charles Wesley

One of the most significant aspects of any threshold covenant is the cornerstone on which it is made. This is quite hard to spot in the Red Sea story. Possibly because it's back in Egypt, where the lintels and doorposts were painted with blood at the Passover. It's even harder to spot during the threshold covenant between God and Abraham.

At first sight, there seems to be very little difference between God's promise on that occasion and any previous time. However, it now included a precise time: *in the time of life, you will be the father of a son to be called Isaac.*

The cornerstone is verbally created in this promise. While the *cornerstone* to catch the sacrificial blood is 'kaph' in Hebrew, the general word for *stone* is ''eben'.

Now this is the first threshold covenant between man and God alluded to in Scripture.[57] It's the threshold of thresholds, as it were.

God Himself creates the stone—by speaking over it the words of promise. These words are about *father* and *son*, here in this *house.*

Father: *ab*

Son: *ben*

Many rabbis have noted ''eben' is effectively formed by overlapping *ab* for 'father'[58] and *ben* for 'son'. The place of overlap is the letter 'b', which in Hebrew is *beth*, the house.

The word ''eben' is therefore meant to convey an understanding that the *foundation stone* of the family is *father and son sharing the same house*.

And in case you are concerned about the ultra-masculine overtones of all this, please note the gender of ''eben' is feminine, signifying woman as the glue holding the house together as a home.

Here ''eben' couples the concept of a *spiritual foundation stone* with *a unity of father and son*. There is no separation in Jewish thinking of spiritual and material. They are not divisible into separate realms: a physical object can be the manifestation of a spiritual reality.

Isaiah exhorts those who seek righteousness: *look to the rock from which you were hewn and the quarry from which you were dug* when reminding the Hebrew people of their heritage as children of Abraham and Sarah.[59] Admittedly the word used by Isaiah is not ''eben', but it has that outlook to it.

For Christian believers Isaiah's words are more profound still: look to Abba Yahweh and His son Yeshua who, in sharing the same house, are truly the foundation stone of the world.

In fact, as we look back to Jesus we see a mirror reflection of the name covenant and threshold covenants between Abraham and God.

Jesus and his little band of disciples had travelled north to Caesarea Philippi, a town in the shadow of Mount Hermon. A temple of Pan in a grotto there allegedly indicated the gateway to hell. At this spot, Jesus turned to His disciples and quizzed them about His identity. He asked first of all who other people thought He was and finished up with a question about who *they* thought He was. 'Who do men say I am?' soon became 'Who do *you* say that I am?'

Simon took the plunge, becoming the first of the disciples to acknowledge Jesus as the Messiah.

Jesus then said some words that have been the subject of repeated controversy over the last two thousand years: *You are Peter and on this rock I will build My church ...*

Now, whatever interpretation of Jesus' words you subscribe to, let me make a point almost universally overlooked: this is a name covenant. Not only a new name but also a covenant. Jesus had just given Simon the name Cephas, derived from 'kaph'—the basinstone which caught the blood of a threshold sacrifice.

And, of course, because it is a name covenant, drawing Simon into unity with God whose name is 'the Rock', it has blessings to go with it.

Cephas does not mean the same as Peter. In *God's Poetry*, I have noted that Peter has the sense of *a stone marking the beginning of an enterprise.*[60] Cephas, on the other hand, is from 'kaph', *the basinstone of the threshold sacrifice*. They have similar but not identical overtones.

In *God's Panoply* I noted the new enterprise began when Peter confessed Jesus as Lord. The foundation of the church was laid—to be followed by living stones linked to this first stone. The words of Jesus, 'On this rock I will build My church,' constitute the moment of conception.

It's a threshold moment but the ratification of the covenant was still to come. Some scholars believe Peter made this statement of faith on the Day of Atonement. Six days later would coincide with the Day of Tabernacles, so Peter's question on the Mount of Transfiguration about building shelters is not as thoughtless as it seems. He might not have known what he was saying but there was a prophetic depth to it, one that not only goes back to the time of Abraham but features many subtle parallels.

God visits Abraham at Mamre	Jesus at Caesarea Philippi and the Mount of Transfiguration
God previously initiates a name covenant with Abram through a revelation of Himself as El Shaddai.	Jesus previously initiates a name covenant with Simon through a revelation of Himself as Messiah.

The name exchange is implicit: Abram does not appear to bestow a new name on God at this point (though he does so explicitly later at Mount Moriah) but God bestows a new name on him.	The name exchange is evident: Simon bestows the title of 'Messiah' on Jesus and Jesus bestows a new name on Simon.
Abram becomes Abraham, a name embodying God as HaShem, the Name.	Simon becomes Cephas/Peter, a name embodying God as the Rock.
Several days after instituting the name covenant between Himself and Abraham, God self-reveals as a man when He visits Mamre, flanked by two heavenly beings—angelic sentinels.	Six days after instituting the name covenant between Himself and Peter, Jesus self-reveals as God at the transfiguration, while flanked by two heavenly beings—Moses and Elijah.
God talks about Abram's son whom He will one day ask to be offered up on Mount Moriah.	God talks about His only-begotten son who is shortly to be offered up on Golgotha—identified as Mount Moriah.
The heirs of the promise are implied in the conversation: the Children of Israel for which God has just laid the foundation stone by His words about Isaac.	The heirs of the promise are implied in the conversation: the church for which Jesus has just laid the foundation stone by His words to Peter.

Within 'the time of life' (probably an allusion to the human gestation period of nine months), the heir is born to much delight and merriment: Isaac means *he laughs.*	Within nine months, the heir—the church—is born at Pentecost to much merriment.
God and Abraham partake of a threshold covenant and also a salt covenant.	Jesus gives Simon a threshold name and obviously initiates a covenant at some point in the six days.
A threshold covenant implies that God and Abraham have become each other's covenant defenders (as well as that of their families—witness the episode with Lot straight after), through the covenant promises exchanged.	Jesus indicates He has become Peter's covenant defender (and the church's as well) when He announces that the keys of the Kingdom of Heaven have been handed over and the gates of hell will not prevail against the church.
The word ''eben', *stone*, has the sense of the father and son sharing the same house (which in the days of the patriarchs would have been a tent.)	Peter suggests building booths—temporary houses—which were to replicate tent living: he almost got the idea—if only he'd suggested the Father and Jesus sharing one tent!
As Abraham and God walk together after the announcement about a son, God shares unusually and frankly with Abraham.	As Peter, James and John walk with Jesus after God's announcement about His son, Jesus shares unusually and frankly with them.

Mamre means *from seeing, from a vision.*	On the Mount of Transfiguration, the disciples saw a vision.
Mamre is near Hebron where the traditional gateway to the Garden of Eden was located. Hebron is one of the last refuges and strongholds of the sons of Anak who were descended from the half-angelic Nephilim.	Hermon is near Caesarea Philippi, where the traditional gateway to Hades was located; Mount Hermon was the traditional site where the fallen angels descended before they become the ancestors of the Nephilim.
The second covenant Abram cut with God was at Mamre near Hebron.	The first covenant Abram cut with God was said to have been undertaken on the slopes of Mt Hermon.
Abraham's covenant relationship with God was contingent upon faith which was counted to him as righteousness.	Peter's covenant relationship with Jesus was contingent upon the faith he expressed just prior to the moment of threshold.

The transfiguration is far more than a revelation of the glory of God in the person of Jesus. I believe the event took place on Hermon, rather than Mount Carmel. Jesus had to go to Mount Hermon at some point to fulfil the prophecy of Psalm 82:1 ESV: *God has taken His place in the divine council ...*

The heights of Zaphon, *the mountain of the north,* is the traditional site of the 'assembly of the gods' or 'divine council'. Here the pantheon of Canaanite gods was said to meet. I believe that, not only should Zaphon be identified with Mount Hermon but also that Jesus, at His transfiguration, directly challenged these gods.

He trampled Python on Python's home turf.

This was a watershed moment. It was the creation of a foundation stone, an ″eben’, for the church itself. A church yet to be born but which would arrive at ‘the time of life’.[61]

It also reflects the moment God came to covenant with Abraham and spoke into life the foundation stone of his lineage through Isaac.

That event in turn reflects the establishment of the foundation stone of all creation. Jewish tradition locates this rock in Jerusalem. This foundation stone is called ‘eben ha-shetiyah, *the rock from which the world is woven*.

You knit me together in my mother's womb ... I am fearfully and wonderfully made ... my frame [foundation stone] was not hidden from You when I was being made ... in the depths of the earth. Your eyes saw my unformed substance [unwoven stone] ...

Psalm 139:13–16 NIV with alternatives

Let's put this threshold covenant which Jesus instituted in context.

He'd come to the town of Caesarea Philippi with his disciples. It's worth taking a brief excursion into some regional geography and history here, otherwise we'll miss the hidden layer in His words when He undertakes the name covenant with Simon.

Caesarea Philippi was named after Philip the Tetrarch, son of Herod the Great and Cleopatra of Jerusalem.

Philip's mother, Cleopatra of Jerusalem, is an obscure, shadowy figure. She may be identical with her famous contemporary, Cleopatra of Egypt, who was Herod's rival. An early case of the maxim: *Keep your friends close and your enemies closer*.

The massive desert fortress of Masada was originally built by Herod to keep an eye on Cleopatra of Egypt. She had been given shared rights with him for a monopoly on extracting asphalt from the Dead Sea. Just in case her political ambitions extended further into his kingdom, he wanted counter-assault forces ready at a moment's notice.

Masada indicates just what level of threat he felt she constituted.

Apart from the mines at the Dead Sea, Cleopatra was also given the territory around Panias in 36 BC. Panias is the very same place which, thirty-three years later, was to become Caesarea Philippi.

Situated on the south-western base of Mount Hermon, Panias was named after the Greek god Pan. At a spring-fed grotto dedicated to him, an entrance to the underworld was believed to exist: the Gates of Hell.

About five kilometres away, there was an ancient shrine of the Israelites: the infamous high place which Jeroboam set up in Dan. There a golden bull calf had been worshipped for centuries, installed by the descendents of Jonathan, grandson of Moses. The original name of Dan was Laish.

Blotting out the near horizon is snow-covered Mount Hermon which, as I have said, I believe is also Zaphon, *the heights of the north*, and abode of the Canaanite gods. It is the first place in Israel to welcome the dawn—the first place which the light of the sun hits each morning. It's a threshold place in its own right. Doubly so, because here, according to the Book of Enoch—a text immensely popular in first century Galilee and quoted in the New Testament—the fallen angels first descended to earth. It was from here they spread out to take for themselves wives from amongst the daughters of men.

Now, with this background in mind, let's look at Matthew 16:18-19 NIV where Jesus institutes the name covenant with Simon: '*I tell you that you are Peter, and on this rock I will build my church, and the gates of Hades will not overcome it. I will give you the keys of the Kingdom of Heaven; whatever you bind on earth will be bound in heaven, and whatever you loose on earth will be loosed in heaven.*'

This is such a contentious statement in the divide between Catholics and Protestants and has been raked over so often and so minutely in the past five centuries, you'd think there'd be nothing more to find. But the problem with having a theological agenda while looking at Scripture is we're very likely to miss anything that doesn't fit neatly into our pre–determined box.

Let's pick out some key words. Whoops, that pun wasn't intentional, unlike some of the following:

Peter: the Greek word is 'petros', which we learn from John 1:42 is actually the Hebrew name Cephas, from 'caph', *cornerstone*, the hollowed–out rock which caught the blood of a threshold sacrifice.

Rock: the Greek word here is 'petra', *pebble*. Ignoring the entire Protestant–Catholic controversy at this point, let's note something curious: this is part of the name Cleopatra, the former owner of the region.

Keys: the Greek word here is 'kleis'. From it we derive the name ... yes, you've probably guessed it: Cleo,[62] again as in Cleopatra.

Church: the Greek word is 'ekklesia', meaning *an assembly* or *calling out*. But take careful note of its centre, 'kles': it's probably another pun on *keys*.

Gates: the concept of 'gates' in Hebrew is synonymous with judges and judgment—in the ancient world, judges sat at city gates. The Hebrew word for *judge* is Dan, the name of a nearby shrine.

Hades: the god of the underworld, the ruler of hell. The Hebrew word for 'hell' is Sheol, related to the name Saul.

Gates of Hades: a pun on the name referring to the grotto of Pan and to spiritual judges, as famously mentioned in the 'divine council' of Psalm 82. The divine council in Ugarit mythology[63] meets on nearby Mount Hermon.

Keys of the Kingdom of Heaven: the name Cleopatra has been variously translated *glory of the fatherland* or *keys of the fatherland*. Let's note the Scripture quote above comes from Matthew 16:18–19 and that Matthew, a Jew with obvious respect for the name of God, universally used the phrase 'Kingdom of Heaven' where Luke used 'Kingdom of God'. Since I suspect Jesus actually spoke these words in Aramaic, I wonder if his original statement was about the keys of the Father's kingdom, thus obliquely referencing Cleopatra's name? And was the wording so clever it worked as a pun in three languages: Greek and Latin as well as Aramaic? In Hebrew, 'peter' is *firstborn* or *one who opens the way*. While 'petros' is translated *rock*, it's obviously a cognate for Cephas, *the cornerstone on the threshold*. 'Petra' is a feminine word, appropriate if it is indeed part of the pun on Cleopatra. However, it seems also to be a pun on 'patria', which is both Greek and Latin for *fatherland*.

Bind: the Greek word is 'deo'. In Aramaic, it is 'kaphath' which suggests it's related to 'kaph', *the cornerstone.*

Loose: tempting to suggest that English *loose* ultimately derives from Greek 'luo', *loose*, but I can't find the etymology of *loose* beyond the thirteenth century. However, in flagging this possibility, I want to note that Laish, the original name of the city of Dan, was pronounced *loosh*. Furthermore, *loose* in Hebrew is 'sharah', related to 'sha'ar', *gate*, and thus doubly evocative of 'dan', *judge*.

The stunning intricacy of interlaced puns in Jesus' statement covers three languages simultaneously. And its incredible, constantly–overlooked aspect is its continual references to the landscape and its history.

I ask myself why.

Yet, as I look at the ultimate end of the story of the woman of Bethlehem who was raped and killed in Gibeah—the dying of the land during the reign of David—I think I understand a secondary aspect of what Jesus was doing in His own threshold inauguration.

He was healing the land.

The land cannot be healed until people are healed and people cannot be healed until the land is healed.

John Loren Sandford

The significance of Jesus' words in speaking the church into life would become apparent within nine months at Pentecost. The significance of His healing the land would take longer.

Naturally the two were connected: the healing of the land, specifically this land in Northern Israel, would intimately impinge on the health of the early church.[64]

There's a pun in Jesus' words which we've yet to consider: the phrase '*Gates of Hades*' could be translated back into Hebrew as the '*judges of Sheol*' or even the '*judgments of Saul*'.

One of the earliest and most dangerous opponents of Christianity was the fanatical Pharisee, Saul of Tarsus. His judgmental nature was accompanied by an extreme fire-breathing passion to see the church destroyed.

As it happened, Saul had to pass through the region of Caesarea Philippi on his way to Damascus. He may not have gone to the town itself but he couldn't avoid the general area. His mission, backed by the authority of the Sanhedrin—the rulers and judges of Israel—was to destroy the nascent church in the north. He was to arrest every Christian he could find in Damascus.

How was Saul to know it was dangerous for him personally to cross the land Jesus had healed? How was he to know his judgments could not possibly stand when Jesus had spoken such a specific blessing into the area he was passing through?

There was a name covenant in operation—and it definitely wasn't Saul's. In fact Saul, though he could not have known it until much later, was approaching his own threshold. In the shadow of Mount Hermon, he saw a blinding light and heard a voice from heaven.

This was where Simon, newly named Peter, had just a year or two earlier also encountered a blinding light and heard a voice from heaven. Jesus was revealed in His transfigured glory to both of them.

When Saul finally got back to Jerusalem, over a decade later, perhaps they compared notes.

This event is the pivotal point of Saul's life. His personal threshold moment. No wonder puns for the various names of Mount Hermon and for the aspects of threshold covenant recur so often in Paul's writings.

Especially when it comes to the armour of God.

Paul, after all, was only following Jesus' lead in a wordplay so dazzling and sophisticated in its pageantry, it almost defies description.

4

'It's complicated.'

ONE SUNDAY MORNING while driving to church I was moaning to God. I'd helped organise a conference and, as one of the coordinators, was responsible for the financial loss. My share was going to amount to a few thousand dollars.

'I checked with You so many times,' I told God. 'I thought You said this was right. I thought You were going to protect us financially. I don't know how I'm going to afford this.'

'If you knew what we were up against,' He replied, 'you'd think this was a very good outcome.'

The voice of God was very clear that morning but I was stunned at what He'd said.

'What? Aren't You God? What do You mean: "what we were up against"?' I was baffled. 'What has any enemy got to do with this? Is anything too hard for You? Aren't You, you know, all-knowing, all-powerful, almighty ... omnipotent, omniscient, omnipresent ... all those 'omni' words?'

'It's complicated.'

It was fortunate I didn't have anything to choke on at that point. 'Complicated!? What do you mean "complicated"?' *What could possibly be 'complicated' for God?*

'Answer coming up in the next five minutes.'

This is the only time in my life when God promised an answer in a very definite time frame so I was very alert. In the next five minutes I arrived at church and the service began. The first of the day's readings was Psalm 82 from the Australian Prayer Book:

God has stood up in the council of heaven: in the midst of the gods He gives judgement.

'How long will you judge unjustly: and favour the cause of the wicked?

'Judge for the poor and fatherless: vindicate the afflicted and oppressed.

'Rescue the poor and needy: and save them from the hands of the wicked.

'They do not know, they do not understand, they walk about in darkness: all the foundations of the earth are shaken.

'Therefore I say, 'Though you are gods: and all of you children of the Most High,

'Nevertheless you shall die like a mortal:
and fall like one of the princes.'

Arise, O God, and judge the earth:
for You shall take all nations as Your possession.

I knew immediately it was God's answer. I didn't understand the Psalm but I typed it out and taped it next to my computer for years. Over time, I realised God had been right about a 'very good outcome'. I watched other people organise very similar conferences and go down financially: thirty thousand dollars, fifty thousand dollars—and, in one spectacular disaster, a quarter of a million dollars. Clearly, whatever we were 'up against' was formidable. But my first question was still unanswered: *So what?* Did it matter how formidable the enemy was? Where was God's protection in all this?

Why was it, according to God's own testimony—if I'd heard right—'complicated'?

I asked but didn't get any answers. In retrospect, I had way too many false refuges getting in the way. In addition, I had a mental conflict. Everyone I respected had one consistent piece of advice when it came to spiritual warfare: *Don't go up against principalities.*

Right, I'd agree, *but there are people named after principalities. They behave as if they have name covenants with dark spiritual powers and are desperate to have those covenants annulled. 'Don't go up against principalities' is just not sufficient in these circumstances.*

For years I prayed God would show me how to deal with principalities, even as I inched my way forward helping to deal with name covenants for many people. Name covenants opened the way to threshold covenants and, as I worked with Christians who wanted to overcome both, we realised that inheritance and healing of the land was entwined with these covenants as well. Searching Scripture confirmed the links between them all.

Complicated?

That hardly begins to describe their complexity.

False refuges; name covenants; threshold covenants with their guards, seals and stone; inheritance and land—one by one they yielded to the Cross of Christ but I still didn't have a clue how to deal with principalities. Whenever I had to deal with a name covenant and the associated principality, I'd say to God, 'I haven't got a clue what to do. But I've just thought of a cool idea. What do You reckon? Is it ok to pray like this?'

I was once asked to pray for two sections of land in another country. There were clear threshold covenants involved in both cases and, in one of them, a name covenant. Since it was a twelve-hour drive from one property to the next, I decided to use the opportunity to indulge in a spot of tourism. It wasn't a very organised trip. Rather it was what the locals call a 'Tiki Tour'—an unplanned scenic drive from one town to the next with spontaneous stops en route.

My Canadian friend Lisa came with me. Our vague plan was to visit a well-known mountain at some point during the trip. Lisa wanted prayer for her own property and this peak happened to share a name with the mountain her land overlooked. On the off-chance there was a name covenant operational, we thought we'd check it out. Perhaps even say a prayer or two.

It didn't dawn on me for a second God had been preparing this moment for over fifteen years.

Time was running short so we thought we'd engage a tour guide to take us up the mountain. We were so glad we did. The guide gave us information we'd never have discovered otherwise.

In the Bible, 'high places' are repeatedly mentioned and, unsuspecting, we had driven right up to one. The spiritual atmosphere was palpable. I felt as if my brain had been slammed into next week and was ricocheting around trying to find its way back to the present. I'd had a 'vision' concerning the spirits at this place fifteen years before (which even included an identifying name) but I'd never taken it seriously.

It took weeks to unravel the information we gained there. There were covenants that affected not only places with the same name but also the entire nation. In the process of sifting through the information we'd been given, it became clear some very high level cosmic powers were involved. In Paul's hierarchy given in Ephesians 6, this group of cosmic powers was at the top: *kosmokrators* or world rulers ranked above principalities.

I was appalled. I didn't know how to deal with a single principality and here, it was clear, God was calling me and a tiny prayer group of bewildered women to do something right then and there. In researching the Biblical precedent for the situation, I realised a fourteen–year gameplan was in play, with a matter of days left until the final assault.

I like to quote Isaiah 28:16, '*Those who believe will not be in haste,*' to all and sundry. So, to me, the urgency of the problem was a huge confrontation in itself. 'We can't do this!' I told God. 'We're not prayer warriors who do huge intercessory things. We have no idea what we're doing. Why us? Why?'

Eventually He was to give me a really curious answer. 'You've repeatedly answered yourself as to why. Because you have no idea what you're doing. You always admit that just before you submit one of your wild plans for dealing with a principality for My approval.'

Wild plans? When had I ever asked God's approval? 'You mean, asking if it's ok to pray a certain way is like submitting a plan for approval?' It was such a mind–blowing revelation I wasn't sure I'd heard right. It was too simple. 'You mean other people don't ask if it's ok?'

'Not often.'

I thought about my wild plans. Some of them were obviously Holy Spirit-inspired (in retrospect, how to get rid of Python and Rachab from a threshold or clearing Leviathan off an inheritance had Scriptural support) but others had always seemed seriously dodgy. Had God sanctioned them simply because I'd asked if it was ok to go ahead with them? For no better reason than I'd had the courtesy to ask what He thought?

This seemed an absurd thought until I read John Paul Jackson's *Needless Casualties of War* and Ken Legg's *Grace to Reign*. There I became aware of how often Christians charge into high-level battle without consulting God at all.

It wasn't as if He'd dropped down a flashing neon banner from the sky with '*Yes!*' on it whenever I'd asked Him about a particular way of proceeding. I don't have a seer anointing. I don't often get visions. I don't hear God especially well. My gift is a sense of pattern—an ability to notice recurring symbols or words.[65] So when a solution occurred to me, more often than not, I'd said to God, 'I'm not sensing a "no" here, so I'll tiptoe forward and, if I'm mistaken about how You want me to proceed, please alert me the moment I'm going wrong.'

I thought I'd been crawling like a spiritual baby for decades. I thought the reason I'd come through so many battles almost totally unscathed was because I was moving slowly and cautiously and, when things looked bad, praying to be hidden in God. Ridiculous when I think about it now. If I was moving as slowly as I thought, I'd have been clobbered to a formless pulp.

I've been clobbered enough times by Python and Rachab in my life to know they weren't going to let me off just because I was praying for someone else, not myself.

It's not rocket science to ask for a divine tick of approval in spiritual warfare. Without it, without the kiss of God lifting us up, we have no armour. '*Don't go up against principalities*' turned out, to my surprise, not to be a rule but a warning. If we haven't asked God about what we're doing then we're like the sons of Aaron who offered unauthorised fire to the Lord.

We are not under His protection or favour as Python, Rachab and Leviathan turn on us with a smug gaze and consider if we've reached the stage of being finger–lickin', lip–smackin' good. Or whether they should wait until that optimum moment when we're fattened so nicely for the kill, it's unlikely—when our world comes crashing down—that we'll ever trust God again.

Christ is our cornerstone
on Whom alone we build;
with His true saints alone
the courts of heaven are filled:
on His great love
our hopes we place
of present grace
and joys above.

Urbs beata Hierusalem, 7th century
trans. John Chandler

When I was writing *God's Panoply*, I was under the distinct impression that, as time went by, the apostle Paul had an increasingly greater revelation of the nature of spiritual armour. For instance, the fact the breastplate of faith and love in 1 Thessalonians 5:8 became a breastplate of righteousness in Ephesians 6:14 seemed indicative of a subtle change in his understanding. This seemed confirmed by the shift in these same verses from the helmet of the hope of salvation to one of outright salvation.

Lately, however, I have moved away from the thought there was an evolution in Paul's thinking. Instead I believe the armour of light is *not* the same as the armour of God: that, just as Persian armour is distinct from Greek armour and Roman armour is different to Celtic armour, there are varieties of spiritual weaponry.

Some is comparatively lightweight, some heavy duty. The ultimate defence system is the armour of God, mentioned in the sixth chapter of Ephesians.

In *God's Panoply*, I suggested there are four layers of meaning hidden in the armour of God. Well, I can now confidently say I was wrong. There are at least eight layers and possibly ten! The four layers I've noted in the past are:

- the surface layer, describing Roman armour
- the immediate sub-surface involving puns in the Greek language on parts of a doorway
- the sub-sub-surface layer which would have been evident to any educated Greek reader involving the mathematical count of letter, word, group and gematria
- the bedrock layer which relies on an understanding that 'to put on armour' is the same word as 'to kiss' in Hebrew

However, there are still other layers: allusions to flowers, gemstones, music and more. Are you thinking with considerable disbelief, 'Yeah, right!?'

Impossible as it seems, the armour of God is a profound and stunning pageant of beauty and majesty. The armour is functional but it's also an artwork! The glory of God as the covenant defender of His people shines out of these verses—so long as you rub them just enough to remove centuries of modernist and post-modernist dust from them.

There are puns, some of them multi-lingual, throughout the description. Of course there are. Jesus used them; why wouldn't Paul?

Let's look at the armour piece by piece, beginning with the helmet of salvation.

Let's also take note of an extremely important point first raised in recent times by Clinton Arnold: the epistle to the people of Ephesus is the only letter of Paul's that does not address itself to a specific issue within the local congregation. In Arnold's view this apparent oversight is nothing of the kind. It was unnecessary to state what the problem was at Ephesus: simply because the whole of the ancient world was aware what bedevilled the city.[66]

Magic.

Ephesus was famous as a centre of sorcery in the first century as well as the worship of multi–breasted Ephesian Artemis.

' ... *we who have fled to Him for refuge can take new courage* ...'

Hebrews 6:18 NLT

Many Christians practise magic unknowingly.

I've already mentioned whirling on the spot whenever I felt troubled as a teenager. I'd totally forgotten this habit until I was researching threshold covenants. The only book on the subject was published in the nineteenth century: Henry Clay Trumbull's *The Threshold Covenant*.

While it's an excellent historical overview, it does not deal with any spiritual aspects: the notion of threshold guardians is beyond its scope, as is any practical way to deal with covenants gone awry.

However, in the age of the internet I don't even have to take myself off to a specialist library to search the entire world for information. Still, the downside to Google is that, in analysing my browsing history, it tailors my searches to make it easier for me to find what I want.[67]

Since I don't know what I want, I'd rather Google didn't narrow my results. I therefore regularly lob in a random term, hoping it will expand the search. Mostly it doesn't.

However, once I threw '*Turkish Delight*' into the mix and hundreds of new pages popped up: all of them on whirling dervishes and Sufism.

At the risk of vast oversimplification, a whirling dervish practices the most visibly–distinctive part of his religion by spinning like a top. His long white robes billow around him as he participates in an ecstacy–inducing communal dance.

The word 'dervish' means *threshold*.

When I first read this, a memory of whirling like a top bubbled up into my consciousness. I recalled spinning and spinning until I felt relief.

Remembering it, I was overwhelmed by a sense of constricting darkness. 'I did something bad, didn't I?' I asked God.

No answer.

I felt impelled to discover what the significance of 'dervish' meaning *threshold* was. The purpose of the dance, according to most websites, is to bring the believer to the point of being able to jump over his own shadow.

This, of course, is impossible in the natural world.

The sense of constricting darkness deepened. I think differently to everyone I know about shadows: *shadows are light's child. They are nothing without the light and nothing if they fall into darkness.*

I had the sudden terrible conviction I'd always wanted to jump over my own shadow. 'Why did I want that?' I asked God.

'The threshold is a perilous place, guarded by powerful watchers. You instinctively knew that, even as a child. So you wanted to leap over it with the aid of magic.'

I felt really sick. It dawned on me that whirling on a threshold is an attempt to counterfeit the wheels of the cherubim.

God wasn't finished. 'Twirling on the spot was your "safe sanctuary" from My calling. Which, by the way, you have *always* rejected.'

I was stunned. 'I'm *not* called to be a writer?'

'No. Not primarily. It's not your main calling.'

For the next two weeks, God left me brooding in what felt like a puddle of poisonous despond. I'm sure He dumped me in it just so I would never ever be in any doubt how He felt about those 'innocent' twirls. They were rebellion of the most monumentally serious kind.

As I've told this story from time to time, I've been surprised to discover this habit of mine is not unique. I've encountered quite a few private twirlers.

Although we constantly seek to create a 'safe sanctuary' for ourselves away from God, all of these places are 'false refuges'.

The first thing we run to when we are disappointed is our false refuge. It can be coffee, food, chocolate, books, shopping, sex, porn, drugs, cigarettes, work, movies, games, social media ... the list is massive and covers hundreds of different possibilities. When I was studying the concept of false refuges through Elijah House prayer ministry training, I have to say I didn't realise twirling should be included. Basically it comes down to anything that distracts us from the disappointment and makes us feel better. Anything that takes the place of God.

We can't deal with any covenants operating in our lives while our false refuges remain intact. And our armour doesn't work inside them.

That's why it's important to renounce them, repent of using them and ask God to demolish them.

His tomb of late the threefold guard
Of watch and stone and seal had barred;
But now in power and triumph high,
He comes from death to victory.

Aurora lucis rutilat, 4th century
trans. John Neale

Besides razing your false refuge with God's help, it's important to understand His sevenfold armour and its properties. It's specifically designed for crossing thresholds. This will become increasingly apparent as we look at it in detail.

There are countless books, articles and sermons available on the panoply of God, examining it in the light of first century Roman armour. It's been done so well in so many places, I'm not going to venture there. I'm only going to boldly go where, as far as I can see, no man has gone ...

... for several centuries.

In *God's Panoply*, I have examined the divine armour in the light of the fact that *to kiss* in Hebrew is the same word as *to put on armour*. The internal evidence clearly suggests that, when Paul told the Ephesians to '*put on the armour of God'*, he was almost certainly expecting them to understand the sub-text: *lift your face for the kiss of God*.

The hallmark of spiritual warfare should not be violence, but courtesy.

We see weapons mentioned, we think *power* and *force*.

We don't think *flowers, gemstones, hospitality, holy kisses*.

It's time we should.

It's time too we realised how much western culture has overlaid a violent veneer on the way we think about spiritual issues. We even call it 'warfare' when really what it's about is 'homecoming'.

We miss the pageantry God has hung over the doorway to welcome us.

Sure we need defence. However, just as we've teetered from one extreme to another over the centuries regarding justice, mercy, truth and peace—promoting one of God's attributes above all others, depending on time, circumstances and cultural inclination—so too we've become unbalanced regarding the armour of God.

And this unbalance all too easily becomes presumption.

One of the functions of God's threshold guardians—the cherubim and seraphim—is to ward off presumption. In a Christian culture where grace is assumed and God's covering is presupposed to be automatic, presumption unfortunately is almost universal.

5

Sevenfold Defence

THE WORD PAUL USES for *helmet* is 'perikephalaia', formed from the prefix 'peri–', *around*, and 'kephale', meaning primarily *head*. It also encapsulates a sense of *supreme, chief, principal, prominent* or *cornerstone*.

In ancient times, the cornerstone was not only the first part of a building laid down, it was also the most sacred place. Situated in the doorway at the corner of a house, the cornerstone formed the threshold. In Hebrew it is 'kaph', a word associated with *atonement*, but in this case meaning *a shallow basinstone* to catch the blood dripping from the lintels and doorposts when a guest was welcomed with a zebihat.

'Kaph' and 'kephale' have something in common.

In fact 'kephale', *head*, comes from 'kapto', a Greek word related to the Hebrew 'kapthor', *crown*.

So Paul's 'perikephalaia' is a helmet with a royal crown, encrusted with glittering wine–red gemstones: garnets.

Garnet comes from the word *pomegranate*. One look inside the fruit and it's obvious why. The pomegranate is a round jewelcase of glistening claret–coloured seeds that look like garnet chips. The cultivated tree has flowers with orange–red ruffles like a flamenco dancer's skirts.

In traditional Jewish culture, the pomegranate is eaten on the first day of the New Year: Rosh Hashanah, *the head of the year*.

Pomegranates were embroidered on the hem of the High Priest's robe, alternating with golden bells. However, they're usually symbolic of the head since 'kaphtor' means both *pomegranate* and *crown*. No doubt influenced by their serrated calyxes which look so crown–like it's said Solomon modelled his coronation circlet after them.

'Kaphtor' was also the name of each of the pomegranate-like decorations atop the two main pillars of Solomon's Temple. Eventually 'kaptor' simply came to mean any ornamental work on the capital of a pillar. Like a lintel on top of a doorway: bringing us back to the idea of zebihat—the threshold welcome shown by the blood-stained lintel.

Allusions to pillars occur in verses 13 and 14: *'Therefore put on the full armour of God, so that when the day of evil comes, you may be able to stand your ground, and after you have done everything, to* ***stand. Stand*** *firm then, with the belt of truth buckled around your waist, with the breastplate of righteousness in place ...'*

Note the word 'stand'—the last word in verse 13 and the first in verse 14. It is 'histemi' in Greek and is derived from 'stuo', *pillar* or *post.*

Isn't this exquisite and poetic? It's an emphasis highlighting the verbal creation of two doorposts.[68]

Before verse 20, Paul will also have alluded to a door, a threshold, a lintel, a hinge and a gate. However, let's return to those later.

His single word 'perikephalaia' is not simply a warrior's headgear. It has deep, subtle allusions to:

- a royal helmet
- a pomegranate flower
- a garnet-studded crown
- a blood-stained lintel

All this—and we haven't even looked at the fact it's a helmet of *salvation*!

Perhaps you're already thinking the multi-layered intricacy of these allusions almost defies belief. And, although we've only glimpsed the first sparkle of the treasure trove and hardly even begun to delve into it, it's worth pausing to ask why it's there.

Why the flowers, the gemstones, the kiss of heaven, the threshold, the covenant and all the rest of the dazzling pageantry of God's panoply? Why?

In my view, it's because this epistle was written to a city of sorcerers. They knew about curses and charms, agreements with demons, gemstone amulets, the power of words, incantations as songs or musical invocations, arcane spells hidden in mathematics[69] or within seemingly nonsensical phrases.

Before the riot in Ephesus instigated by the silversmith Demetrius, recorded in Acts 19, many people turned to Jesus and burned their books of magic. This happened because the seven sons of the Jewish chief priest Sceva tried to cast out demons in the name of Jesus whom Paul preached. In a town like Ephesus where magic was a way of life, there were no doubt many opportunities for a deliverance ministry. The sons of Sceva, however, wound up seriously wounded and having to flee naked from a house when a man with an evil spirit jumped them and demanded, *'Jesus I know and I know about Paul—but who are you?'*

As a result of this notoriety, Paul was able to spread the gospel message much more widely. Many Jews and Greeks repented of dabbling in the occult and threw their scrolls of magic on a huge bonfire. The value of these spells was a staggering fifty thousand drachmas—around 150 years' wages for an average labourer.

Meantime, down in the central business district of Ephesus, the silversmiths were getting agitated. Artisans like Demetrius who made silver shrines and figurines of Artemis found the success of Paul's evangelistic efforts was seriously impinging on their profits. He called his fellow-tradesmen together: *'Men ... you see and hear how this fellow Paul has convinced and led astray large numbers of people here in Ephesus and in practically the whole province of Asia. He says that man-made gods are no gods at all. There is danger not only that our trade will lose its good name, but also that the temple of the great goddess Artemis will be discredited, and the goddess herself, who is worshipped throughout the province of Asia and the world, will be robbed of her divine majesty.' When they heard this, they were furious and began shouting: 'Great is Artemis of the Ephesians!'* (Acts 19:23–28 NIV)

The end result was that Paul was bundled off quickly to Macedonia before he could come to harm. Now, at the end of his life, he's writing back to the converts in this same town—sophisticated, subtle-minded men and women who once valued magic as a means of control and who live in a milieu still dominated by the principalities and powers Paul has repeatedly addressed throughout his letter.

If there's one thing Paul would have been eager to convey, it was how to stand against Artemis—how to take captive every thought, align it to God's word and steer clear of the incantations which summon spirits.

It was therefore necessary to address the question of how God saw gemstones and flowers, music and mathematics, words and seals—all the good things of His creation which had been perverted to magical ends.

So, I believe that when Paul addressed the Christians of Ephesus and instructed them to put on the helmet of salvation, he was also firing another salvo at his old nemesis, Ephesian Artemis.

Many statues of this goddess have been found throughout Asia Minor. They commonly possess a mural crown: a high coronet with ornamentation featuring the walls, ramparts or turrets of a city.

Such regalia amounts to a claim Artemis is worthy to rule, since she is to be considered the defender of any city in which she is worshipped.

By choosing to link helmet and salvation, I believe Paul was refuting this claim by referencing God's promise to His people: *No longer will violence be heard in your land, nor ruin or destruction within your borders, but you will call your walls* 'Salvation' *and your gates* 'Praise'. (Isaiah 60:18 NIV)

Would the people of Ephesus have recognised this allusion?

I think so.

I think there's a strong chance Paul would have already said this when he was in the city itself. Even if he didn't, the people would surely have realised the Holy Spirit had inspired him to describe elegant, intricate multi-layered armour that could deflect absolutely anything unholy sent against it.

Even magic.

Magic.

It seems such a pointless thing to be making a repeated point about, doesn't it? After all, who believes in magic these days?

Most people do.

But most people don't know they do.

It would never have occurred to me twirling on the spot was an attempt to use magic. Just as it would never occur to most Christians some prayers and some prayer practices are actually ritual incantations.

Any prayer with a guarantee that, if it's said correctly for a period of days, you will achieve your desire is simply a magical spell. It doesn't matter whether it's for the conversion of your unbelieving spouse, for the return of your prodigal child to the faith or for the finding of a lost valuable—make no mistake, it's not about the exercise of faith, it's about the performance of magic. It doesn't matter which highly respected Christian teacher advocates the use of such a prayer—it's still not about the exercise of faith, it's really a performance of magic.

Visualisation all too easily crosses the line from faith into magic. If God gives you a picture, it's one thing—if you choose to visualise and repeatedly concentrate on a desired outcome, it's entirely another.

'Name it and claim it' or 'word of faith' practices also cross the boundary into magic way too often for us not to be exceedingly cautious about using them.

Clinton Arnold puts it superbly: 'In religion one prays and requests from the gods; in magic, one commands the gods and therefore expects guaranteed results.'[70]

Even 'standing on the promises of God' as a sure foundation can trespass over the wafer–thin fence–line between faith and magic.

In a prayerful request, God always retains the right to say 'no'. He is still Lord.

If you're going to be so disappointed with a 'no' from God you'd turn your back on Him and walk away, or if you see the promises of God as an iron–clad guarantee for a *specific* situation and not overall for His purposes with the people of God, it's time to take a good hard look at your relationship with Him.

Are you trying to manipulate Him? Are you demanding He fulfill His promises in order for you to have faith in Him?

Or will you follow Him regardless?

Can you say with the friends of Daniel who were about to be thrown into the fiery furnace it doesn't make any difference whether God chooses to save you or not?

Is your faith dependent on God always saying 'yes'?

If it is, then it isn't faith.

On the other hand, if you always expect God to say 'no', that isn't faith either.

You might be exercising faithfulness, but not faith.

The just don't live by faithfulness, they live by faith.

They live by the confidence God will enable them to fulfil the calling He has spoken into the name by which they are called.

There's nothing new in what Paul says about God's armour. In describing it, he was obviously thinking of the scroll of the prophet Isaiah where the Lord Himself has a helmet of salvation. Just a few verses before the walls called 'Salvation' are promised, there is this prophecy:

He put on righteousness as His breastplate, and the helmet of salvation on His head ...

Isaiah 59:17 NIV

The most striking aspect of the surviving statues representing Ephesian Artemis is rarely the mural crown. In fact, the breastwork is such a dominant feature in almost every case it's easy to be distracted by it. Not all statues are the same; however, a common feature is eighteen or so 'breasts'—or bee hives, or ostrich eggs, or bull testicles, or oversized grapes, or sacred acorns. Obviously no one is sure exactly how to interpret the large globular adornments to her torso,[71] though there is general agreement it is a fertility or nurturing symbol of some kind.

In addition, the breastwork on the statues of Ephesian Artemis is hemmed at the top by a band carved with the zodiac.

This is the feature that puts it into direct competition with Aaron's breastplate—the ephod of the Jewish high priest adorned with twelve gemstones representing the twelve tribes of Israel. These twelve tribes were also symbolised in the 'Mazzaroth'—the constellations we call the zodiac.

So back to Isaiah went Paul in his efforts to correct the thinking of the Ephesians: it's important to be girded with the armour God Himself wears, in particular the breastplate of righteousness.

As we have already seen, one word in Hebrew can point to both *breastplate* and *righteousness*: 'sharon' or 'shiryan'.

Another way of interpreting this vital piece of armour is *mailcoat of justice*.

The dispensers of justice in ancient Israel were the judges who traditionally sat in the gates to deliver their judgments. Hence *gates* and *judges* came to be synonymous. So when Jesus said to Simon, at the very moment of renaming him Cephas, *threshold rock*, 'The gates of hell will not prevail against it,' he meant the judges of hell would have to go through Him first to get to the church.

And He won't let that happen.

One of the words for *gates* in Hebrew is 'sha'ar', head-rhyme for 'sharon' or 'shiryan'. This suggests *gate* was meant to evoke justice in people's minds, as the judges of Israel delivered wise and righteous verdicts.

There are several points to note:

If your name is Sharon, it's a threshold name. Part of your calling is to deliver justice; however because this name covenant is also indicative of a threshold covenant, a tangle of problems can arise. When things go wrong, they go badly wrong. Instead of justice, horrific injustice can repeat itself. When there are two covenants operating, it's worth looking for a third—such as a covenant with death—since Satan knows, just as well as we do, that a threefold cord is hard to break.

There are many allusions to an entranceway within the armour of God: we've already noted two pillars and a lintel in the last section. The reference to gates is the only really subtle one; almost all of the others are Greek puns that would have been groaningly obvious to the reader. This wordplay, however, relies on a knowledge of the Hebrew language.

'Gates' suggests something none of the other threshold allusions do. Gates belong to a city, whereas the other entranceway elements could belong to a house. When I first noticed the reference to the gates, I was immediately struck by a possibility that should have occurred to me during the writing of *God's Panoply*, but which I overlooked. The armour of God seems to be for corporate use, rather than individual. It's for the Body of Christ as a whole, not personal application. Indeed, Clinton Arnold verifies this in his commentary on Ephesians 6:18,

'The spiritual warfare passage is often viewed in individual terms; that is, each individual Christian should pray and ask God for strength to do battle. Paul actually depicted the arming in corporate terms. The whole church is involved in the process of arming. All of Paul's admonitions in this passage are plural.'[72]

Indeed Arnold goes so far as to say at one point:

'We are responsible for arming our fellow-believers with the power of God.'

Sharon is twice mentioned in Scripture associated with a flower. As noted in the last chapter, it's the 'chabatstseleth', variously translated in Isaiah[73] and Song of Songs[74] as *rose, rock rose, crocus* or *meadow-saffron*. Although it is commonly suggested 'chabatstseleth' is the daffodil-like narcissus tazetti, the botanical identification matters less than the meaning of the word: *overshadowed by God's love*. How exquisite! This is why I think 'sharon' and 'chabatstseleth' are routinely linked: when justice is not overshadowed by God's love, it can become simple legalism—technicalities of law, rather than a mix of fairness and integrity.

This is one of those rare, rare cases where a pun actually transcends the language barrier. Not the whole pun, with its symphonic complexity, translates from Hebrew to Greek but a fair bit does: Rhoda is a name in

Greek which means *rose* or *rock rose*. In the Book of Acts, Rhoda is recorded as the name of the gatekeeper who was so excited by Peter's miraculous escape from prison she left him still knocking at the door while she argued with the sceptical praying assembly that he was just outside.[75] The comedy of the moment was, I'm sure, irresistible to Luke as he selected what to write about the early days of the church. But equally, I'm sure, the fun of the story was about the names. A Jewish reader of the Book of Acts who encountered the name Rhoda would naturally have thought of a flower connected with a gate—the rose of Sharon—and realised the whole story was indeed one of being 'overshadowed by God's love'.

Jewish readers of the time, however, left to their own devices probably would not have linked *gates* in the first instance to Rhoda. If any name sprang to mind, it should have been Dan, *judge*. Indeed Dan, the fifth son of Jacob, is one of the patriarchs of the twelve tribes of Israel symbolised by the Mazzaroth, *the zodiac*. The counterpart of the zodiac atop the breastwork of Ephesian Artemis was the twelve gemstones on the breastplate of the Jewish High Priest. Dan's gemstone was the *cappiyr*—a blue stone whose name is suggestive of sapphire. However, lapis lazuli was called 'gold-sprinkled sapphire' so *cappiyr* may have been this azure-blue gold-flecked stone worn by the judges of Egypt[76] on gold chains as a symbol of truth. The Israelites were in Egypt long enough for such a connection—*judge* and *lapis lazuli*—to take root in their minds.

The breastwork of Ephesian Artemis carries an entirely different connotation to the breastplate of righteousness. The culture surrounding her worship was one of magic. The purpose of magic is to manipulate and dominate—in essence, to gain an unfair advantage. Righteousness on the other hand is about fairness, uprightness, truth and justice.

Again, Paul's description of divine armour contrasts with that of the 'queen of heaven'.

God is the ultimate upright judge. His fairness is so finely tempered, He will not dismiss any case out of hand without hearing the evidence. Scripture testifies to this repeatedly, yet the implications of this aspect of God's character are almost universally ignored in modern Christian thinking. How just is God? So just and so fair He will even hear the petitions of Satan, the accuser. Until the final Day, He will not send the enemy of our souls off, tail between his legs, without hearing what he has to say against us.

We forget this.

We put ourselves in harm's way whenever we do forget it. We assume we do not have to request our Advocate to appear in the courts of heaven on our behalf.

Yet this is what prayer is all about. It's why we're called to pray for others—because in doing so, we are presenting petitions before the Throne of Grace, asking for the intervention of the blood of Jesus so that a situation changes.

Rebecca Brown suggests it is sometimes necessary to present a counter–petition against Satan's accusations and specifically request our heavenly Advocate to appear on our behalf. Some of Satan's allegations are going to be false but the vast majority are going to be fully justified.

Modern–day western Christianity has a mindset that either dismisses the idea of Satan entirely or else dismisses the idea we need to specifically and intentionally ask for representation. There's a widespread notion that, because of the Cross, Satan's case against us is all dealt with automatically. We tend to think it never gets to court. Our thinking is that our plea bargain, based on the covenant we have with Jesus, is rubber–stamped without any action required on our part.

Does God rubber–stamp anything?

Does God set anything to automatic?

A covenant is about relationship, not about programmed reaction. Any other attitude is perilous.

When we start to assume too much about our relationship with God, we become like Samson. One of the great judges of Israel, he presumed too much on God's protection. Having outwitted the enemy Philistines on several occasions, he got careless. Samson is remembered for his strength but he was brilliantly clever too.

Samson went to Gaza, and there he saw a prostitute, and he went in to her. The Gazites were told, 'Samson has come here.' And they surrounded the place and set an ambush for him all night at the gate of the city. They kept quiet all night, saying, 'Let us wait till the light of the morning; then we will kill him.' But Samson lay till midnight, and at midnight he arose and took hold of the doors of the gate of the city and the two posts, and pulled them up, bar and all, and put them on his shoulders and carried them to the top of the hill that is in front of Hebron.

Judges 16:1–3 ESV

What!? There's a group of killers waiting just outside the gate and, even though taken by surprise, they can't manage to knock Samson off in the thirty kilometre trek from Gaza to Hebron. Even when he can't fight effectively with the gates on his shoulders? It defies credibility!

Actually it is impossible to grasp what's happening in this mysterious episode without an understanding of threshold covenants. While Samson was inside Gaza, the citizens were bound by the code of hospitality integral to a threshold covenant.

In fact the Philistines proved to be vastly more honourable than the people of Benjamin in that tragic story about Gibeah recounted just a few chapters later in the Book of Judges. They wouldn't attack Samson while he was in the city. That would have violated the covenant and called down a deluge of curses on their heads. The Philistines were waiting outside the gates so that, once he left the city, the provisions of the covenant would no longer apply.

Samson, however, picked up the gates and headed for Hebron. There was considerable method in this madness. By carrying the gates, he was extending the city boundaries. While they were on his shoulders, he was effectively still inside the city and the threshold covenant continued to apply. The Philistines were unwilling to lay a hand on him while it did.

Moreover, despite the load he was carrying, Samson headed for distant Hebron. Why Hebron? Perhaps because it was a city of refuge. No doubt as he crested the hill in front of it, guards swarmed to his rescue.

Very clever.

Considerable talk in some Christian circles today revolves about 'possessing the gates of the enemy'. I believe we should exercise extreme caution in this regard. Samson got himself into dire trouble because of a prostitute, then came up with a nifty plan to extricate himself. He failed to learn anything as a result of his possession of the enemy gates. Instead he came to presume that, between his own strength, his own swift intelligence and God's favour, nothing could touch him.

Eventually he reaped what he sowed: it was in Gaza he finally died. Ironically, between two pillars.

His strength and his intelligence were entirely dependent on God's favour. It's a lesson we need to remember, too. The armour of God is a privilege—we should never presume to think otherwise.

The name of the gemstone 'cappiyr' on the breastplate of the high priest is derived from 'caphar', one meaning of which is *covering* or *atonement*. It is related to Cephas, *threshold stone*, the name Jesus bestowed on Simon when he recognised Him as the Messiah.

Both Cephas and Peter allude to *beginnings, first things, embarking* or *arriving*. Even across vast cultural transitions, 'caph' and 'saph' retain that same sense. Safina is a name coming from the Torres Strait islands between Australia and Papua New Guinea. It means *first boat to reach its destination, always arrives safely*.

I have a feeling God watches over sounds to protect their inherent meaning—so that they retain an elemental sense of it, regardless of what we attribute to them.

So, while the allusion to 'cappiyr'—the sapphire or the gold-flecked 'sapphire', lapis lazuli—is altogether subtle, I believe it is there and intentional. This would make it the second reference to a gemstone in the description of the Armour of God.

The first was, of course, *garnet*.

There are twelve gemstones on the High Priest's choshen, *breastplate*. The first of these was odem, meaning *red*. It's basically the same word as Adam, *red*. Often translated *ruby*, *carnelian*, *jasper* or *sard*, I believe this particular jewel, symbolic of the tribe of Reuben, is actually the semi–precious garnet.

Reuben was Jacob's firstborn. It makes sense he would have a colour associated with 'first' and a gemstone associated with 'head'. Garnet, through its relationship with pomegranate, which in Hebrew was called caphtor, *crown*, surely qualifies. Perhaps the tradition of garnet as the 'birthstone' of January is a faint memory of its old prominence.

We saw previously that perikephalaia, *the helmet* of salvation, was not simply the headgear of a warrior but also

- a royal helmet
- a pomegranate flower
- a garnet–studded crown
- a blood–stained lintel

So, too, the thorax is not simply the ancient equivalent of a bulletproof vest but:

- a priestly choshen
- a narcissus or 'rose' of Sharon
- a cuirass decorated with sapphires or lapis lazuli
- gates of truth and judgment

Look over these lists. Kings, priests and judges—that's who we are. Paul hasn't said it outright in this particular passage of his letter to the Ephesians but he's constantly implied it. That's why the armour is like it is: it proclaims our identity as a Christian community and our common destiny.

But that identity is only possible through covenant.

The New Age movement is characterised by a monistic worldview that has much in common with classic Hinduism. Monism is the belief the entire universe is a living unified whole. God permeates the entire universe, and in a sense every person is part of God. God and humanity are therefore one.

Clinton E. Arnold, *Powers of Darkness*

In orthodox Christianity, God and humanity are not one. Jesus' terrible death on the Cross was as a result of God's determination to make a way by which He and humanity might again become one.

The good news of salvation is that Jesus, who is one with the Father, desires to be one with us through the four covenants He instituted.

Four covenants?

Of course four.

Blood, salt, name and threshold—the very same ones Abraham undertook two millennia previously. Abraham's covenants with God occurred over a span of fourteen years; Jesus' covenants with His disciples span a single evening.

And those covenants, making a bridge back to God across the chasm of sin, are the essence of the gospel. Covenant is different to contract because covenant involves oneness. This is the gospel: a way into unity with God exists through faith in Jesus as Lord and Saviour.

Indeed the gospel forms a vital part of the armour of God: '*...your feet shod with the preparation of the gospel of peace ...*' (Ephesians 6:15 KJV)

Many translations have '*shoes of the good news of peace*', though shoes aren't actually mentioned. Instead there's a strange word: 'hupodeo', *underbindings*.

Perhaps we should again look at figurines of Ephesian Artemis to check out the feet. However, before we do, I want to address why we should.

This is not meant as an academic book. The purpose of the theology here is devotional.

If you're reading it for the purpose for which it is intended, you're likely to be a person who thinks, 'I don't need to know about Ephesian Artemis. Paul didn't mention the names of any goddesses, so why should I give them even the slightest attention?'

First, Paul didn't need to mention names because everyone knew. Moreover, Daniel did. In Daniel 11, the 'goddess of fortresses' is mentioned—Chuck Missler suggests this is a reference to the worship of 'Roma'—the city of Rome as a deity in its own right—in Smyrna, not far from Ephesus.[77]

Secondly, you need to know because you're not Moses. God spoke to Moses face to face but, for the rest of us, He explicitly stated He would communicate differently. Some of His ways include:

- prophecy
- dreams
- dark speech /figurative language
- words of knowledge
- words of wisdom
- visions
- logic (though not by itself)
- symbolic action
- discernment of spirits
- conversation with Him

So, when your son has a nightmare, you should be wise enough to ask him about it instead of trying to console him with the thought it's just a bad dream. Suppose he's had a terrifying nightmare about a city of little people who live on his head and want to burrow into his brain. You might be likely to dismiss God's warning unless you happen to think: *city on the head—the goddesses of Asia Minor have crowns like that. And they're counterfeits for the helmet of salvation. I should be putting on the helmet of salvation for* myself, *as well as helping him put his on. Because God's armour is corporate.*

In knowing the symbols of other gods, we can spot the counterfeit and immediately turn to the real. In this case, we'd run straight to El Shaddai, whose name is usually translated *God Almighty* but, as we have seen, is more accurately rendered *the strong-breasted one*. El Shaddai is more about gentle motherly nurture than solid masculine power.

Now both the feet and girdle in many statues of Ephesian Artemis were engraved with magical sigils. The infamous 'Ephesian grammata' were a group of six words—essentially as untranslatable as *abracadabra*—considered to be an immensely powerful incantation.[78] They were known throughout the ancient world as words of power which could control men, spirits and circumstances. In one gladiatorial bout, a contestant was found to have the Ephesian grammata bound around his ankles. After a keen-eyed referee spotted this unfair advantage and the amulet was removed, the gladiator's winning streak was over—he lost the next three bouts.

So, was Paul contrasting the binding spells of the magical grammata with the underbindings of God's spell of peace?

Gospel, after all, simply means *God's spell*.

While I think Paul's motive was indeed to make a contrast with the Ephesian grammata, I also think he had his eye once more on both Isaiah and Song of Songs:

I am the rose of Sharon and the lily of the valleys.

Song of Solomon 2:1 NKJV

How beautiful upon the mountains are the feet of the messenger who announces peace, who brings good news ...

Isaiah 52:7 NRS

In the second verse we've got feet, peace and good news or gospel all wrapped up in one announcement proclaiming that God reigns.

As for that first verse, it links *peace* as the meaning of Solomon to the breastplate of righteousness as well as evoking Jesus' words:

Consider the lilies of the field ... they neither toil nor spin. And yet I say to you even Solomon in all his glory was not arrayed like one of these. Now if God so clothes the grass of the field ... will he not much more clothe you, O you of little faith?

Matthew 6:28–30 NKJV

Is this why Paul talks of underbindings and not shoes? Does he want us to think of things bound to the feet like the Ephesian grammata, as well as flowers underfoot?

I find Paul's choice of word extremely odd. If he was indeed thinking of Roman armour, why did he avoid 'caligulae', *the metal-studded footwear* worn by the imperial troops? On the other hand, perhaps it's not so strange, given the excesses of the Emperor nicknamed Caligula, *little boots*.

But what about 'luo', *shoes*, or 'sandalion', *sandals*?

Now the word 'sandalion' is derived from the name of the god Sandon, the tutelary deity of Paul's hometown, Tarsus, so perhaps it's not so strange either.

The wearing of sandals was banned on Yom Kippur, the Day of Atonement—and *is*, to the present day, amongst observant Jews. Perhaps, since the armour is specially designed for crossing thresholds and 'kippur' derives from 'kaph', *threshold stone*, the so-called 'shoes'[79] cannot be sandals.

Perhaps 'underbinding' is actually subtle advice to take off our shoes because it's holy ground, but still have a layer to separate us from the earth.

To summarise, the 'shoes of the gospel of peace' point to:

- a message of victory over the powers
- a lily symbolising peace and provision
- an alabaster floor underfoot
- God, the foundation

Alabaster? Foundation? Where did they come from?

In Greek, the word for God is not 'I am' with its overtones of the eternal. Instead it is the enigmatic 'theos', related to *foundation*.

God. The word, I mean. The word '*God*'.

Does it mean the same as Yahweh? No, actually it doesn't.

Does it mean the same as 'theos'? No, it doesn't either.

Does 'theos' mean the same as Yahweh? Even that's pretty tricky. Almost certainly not.

Does any of this matter?

In *God's Panoply*, I made the point—which I'm making here again—it is perilous to translate from one language to another and assume the entire symphony of meaning comes along with it. We need to take extra care with Scripture, because the New Testament is already a translation and, unless we're very careful, we're going to have casualties along the way.

English is a mongrel language. An interweaving of Norman–French and Anglo–Saxon after 1066 meant there were often distinct words for similar things. This was particularly so when it came to food: cow and beef, for instance, sheep and mutton, deer and venison, calf and veal.

By 1611, this fusion of traditions ensured the translators of the King James Bible—the 'Authorised Version' of the Scriptures—had quite a number of choices available to them to signify the supreme deity.[80] They selected the word 'God': which doesn't derive from 'good' though it has the singular advantage of looking like it does.

It's said to be able to be traced back through a Gothic word to Sanskrit and basically mean *the one invoked* or the *one sacrificed to*. Now when we use the English word 'God', it's all too easy to default to this kind of understanding. We can be a bit like the Israelites at the foot of Mount Sinai: *so the God who has rescued us from Egypt is Yahweh—'I am who I will be who I am who I was.'*[81] *Hmm, bit of a mind–warping mouthful. Let's try 'the ever–living one'. Of course! We've got it. His symbol must be a calf. That's what our erstwhile Egyptian masters used to signify the ever–living reborn sun.*

The golden calf isn't an aberration: it's a transfer of a pre–existing mindset.

Because different words for God are fused into different names (and name covenants), it's a significant issue. To blithely assume all gods are equal is a modern western conceit. It lacks intellectual substance but that hasn't stopped a lot of highly intelligent people adopting the view.

In *The Last Battle*, the seventh book of *The Chronicles of Narnia*, the Calormene officer Emeth is discovered inside the 'stable' of faith. The character is probably as stunned as the readers when Aslan reveals Emeth's worship of the carrion god Tash has been accepted as worship of the Great Lion and the Emperor–over–Sea.

As a consequence of this scene, CS Lewis has often been accused of believing in universal salvation—though it's clear from what happens to the dwarves, Susan and the vast bulk of the Calormenes this is not the case.

I believe Lewis was making the point that using the right name for God is no guarantee our hearts are actually worshipping Him. Nor that using the wrong name for God automatically consigns us to the company of those who don't know Him.

Yet names are important.

Names that encode 'god' elements, particularly so.

In *God's Poetry*, I looked at names like Hugh and Owen and what it means that they ultimately derive from either Jesus or the bloodthirsty Teutonic god Hesus—or an entanglement of both.

People coming out of witchcraft are likely to ask cautiously, 'Which Jesus?' as they are encouraged to pray to the Father in the name of Jesus. Paul talked about those who preach 'another Jesus'—yet the widespread view of Christians is that this is a warning about theological error, not about a demon that has adopted the name 'Jesus'.[82]

Can't happen?

Yet Jesus Himself was constantly reclaiming names of God that had been adopted by spirits in the demonic realm. Names like 'The Light of the World' which had been taken by Mithras, a favourite god of the Roman legions. Or 'The Bread which comes down from heaven', a title usurped by the Chaldean harvest–god, Tammuz. Or 'The True Vine', a name nabbed by Dionysius, a Cretan god whose worship was so horrific it was banned by the Romans. His revels included rape, murder and mutilation as party–goers dared each other to show how wild and amoral they could be.[83]

What's your mind–set like?

Is it affected by the covenant over your name?

Which Jesus are you worshipping?

Is the intention of your heart (which happens to be deceitful and wicked above all things and might just be concealing things from you) the same as the intention of your mind?

One of the very last letters we have of Paul's is his second epistle to Timothy. He wrote it from prison and a sense of foreboding pervades it. Paul seems conscious this may be his final chance to impart instruction to his 'son in the faith'.

In many ways, while the letter does have a series of reminders and exhortations, it also resembles a deathbed blessing; those prophetic words a father speaks into the lives of his sons and daughters, as Jacob did when he proclaimed the destiny of his twelve sons and their descendants.

To speak properly into a child's life and propel him into his true destiny, you empower his name and ensure the right covenant is operational. Jacob didn't get this from Isaac, which may have been why he took so much trouble with his own children.

There's a great deal in this epistle to Timothy that qualifies in regard to name, blessing and covenant, but it's probably best summed up in just a few verses of the second chapter:

Nevertheless, God's solid foundation stands firm, sealed with this inscription: 'The Lord knows those who are His,' and, 'Everyone who confesses the name of the Lord must turn away from wickedness.' In a large house there are articles not only of gold and silver, but also of wood and clay; some are for noble purposes and some for ignoble. If a man cleanses himself from the latter, he will be an instrument for noble purposes, made holy ...

2 Timothy 2:19–21 NIV

Everything there is a blessing over the name Timothy.

This comes from 'Timotheos' meaning *God–honouring* or *honoured by God* and is derived from 'timao', *to honour* and 'theos', *god*. Other names which encode 'theos' are Dorothy, Theodore, Matthew and the like.

Most concordances offer Strong's opinion that the derivation of 'theos' is uncertain. Greek–speaking people today often equate it with 'theein', *to run*,[84] supposedly meaning 'all people run to God for protection.'

Many scholars, however, offer the opinion that 'theos' is derived from 'tithemi', meaning to *appoint, put, ordain, set in place, lay horizontally, bow down, prostrate, set forth (in the sense of explain—hence the modern derivative 'thesis'*[85]*), fix, establish.*

The name of the Greek goddess of law and justice, Themis, is related to 'tithemi' since customs, laws and rights were those things set firmly in place.

The word 'tithemi' is also related to 'themelios', *foundation.*

I'm inclined to go with 'theos' as a derivative of 'tithemi', *appoint.* Partly because the contemporary Jewish historian Josephus uses a very odd expression for 'children of God': *children of Seth.* Seth is Hebrew for *appointed*, suggesting 'theos' means the same.

Moreover Paul continually used the evocative 'themelios', *foundation*, in his letters to Timothy and the Ephesians. In fact, he seriously mixes his metaphors in Ephesians when he does.[86]

Since, according to tradition, Timothy was martyred at Ephesus after protesting the worship of Artemis, this suggests Paul was speaking specifically and prophetically into Timothy's ministry there.

He's activating the destiny encoded in Timothy's name—as a father is called to do.

But there's more.

This is Paul, after all. Master of the subtle allusion. If he can work seven flowers and gemstones, a kiss and a musical signature into the wording of the armour of God, he won't be holding back here.

The other immensely significant Greek word related to 'tithemi' is 'diatheke', *covenant*. Diatheke comes from a combination of 'dia', *two*, and 'tithemi', *to place*.

It's a word picture of the covenant ceremony: two people standing in place, in a pool of blood, invoking blessings and curses, exchanging identities, destinies and defence in the threefold transfer of names, mantles and weapons. It speaks of that irrevocable decision that brings the two parties into 'oneness'.

Paul's subtle references to a covenant spill out all over these verses. Specifically, he refers to the threshold or cornerstone covenant. And he adds specific warnings.

Every name encodes a choice.

You can come into the destiny God has planned for you or you can chart your own.

In this case, Paul warns Timothy against trampling on God's cornerstone, the age–old signal of refusing hospitality and insulting the one offering it. He achieves this with a single word in the phrase: '*some are for noble purposes and some for ignoble.*'

The word for 'ignoble' means *trampling on the blood of the altar stone and dishonouring the sacrifice*.

In the passage, Paul has conflated two ideas: the cornerstone of which Isaiah spoke with its inscription, '*Those who believe will not be in haste*,' and the foundation stone of the world, the ''eben ha–shetiyah', *the stone from which the world was woven.*

Timothy, like Thea and Dorothy, Theodore and Matthew, are names that honour God as Rock.

At least that's what they're meant to do.

We've always got a choice.

As enemies, we can trample on the Rock. As friends, we can be just as insulting and smite it twice. Or we can simply be indifferent.

While this choice might apply most especially to those of us with 'theos' embedded in our names, in truth, it applies to everyone.

As Paul tells Timothy, to do it right, we must cleanse ourselves for noble assignments.

Those assignments the divine Poet created us for, and appointed for us to undertake before the world began.

Paul had a sharp sense of humour. After the shoes of the gospel of peace, he mentions the shield of faith with which to deflect the fiery darts of the evil one.

The word he uses for *shield*, 'thureos', comes from 'thura', *door.*[87]

The word he uses for those fiery *darts*, 'belos', is a pun on 'belos', *threshold.*

Yep, same word.

The Greek readers would have got the joke instantly. They might have missed the one about the gates and the breastplate of righteousness which relied on a knowledge of Hebrew, but there's nothing subtle here. This reference to the threshold of a doorway is also indicative of a cornerstone covenant.

Furthermore it mentions fiery darts, indicating an attack on the threshold. Python, Rachab and Leviathan don't intend to let us pass without a fight.

Straight off, these fiery darts tells us the cornerstone covenant has something very wrong with it. Instead of angel escorts welcoming us into our destiny, we've taken a serious hit.

This means major spiritual renovation regarding its seals, bindings and foundation needs to be done.

Have you noticed Paul has already mentioned bindings and also alluded to foundations while discussing footwear? He built up a highly integrated imagery in referring to a threshold.

Before looking more closely at the doorway, I want to take a short interlude to highlight the hidden gemstones and flowers here on its verge.

Up to now, a flower and a gemstone have been coded together:

- pomegranate flower & garnet
- rose of Sharon & lapis lazuli
- lily & alabaster

Both lily-of-the-valley and rose of Sharon are mentioned in the same verse of Song of Songs. So Paul's got a truly lovely segue of thought here. Moreover *lily* and *alabaster* combine in the single word, 'shesh', which also means *linen*.

It's a pity alabaster is not one of the gems to be found on the choshen of the High Priest. At least as far as we know. Many of the twelve stones are difficult to identify with any surety.

What flower represents faith? Surely the golden-petalled flower of the mustard bush. Jesus after all said to his disciples: '*I assure you, even if you had faith as small as a mustard seed you could say to this mountain, "Move from here to there," and it would move. Nothing would be impossible.*' (Matthew 17:20 NLT)[88]

And the gemstone? My guess is that it's either a pearl or white agate.

In Hebrew there's a word for *shield*, 'tsinnah', which also means *coldness of snow*. Hence my choice of something white. Ice-coloured agate or chalcedony is the third foundation stone in John's vision of the heavenly Jerusalem. However, each gate—basically each doorway—in his vision is a single massive pearl.

And while John's vision was far too late to have any influence on Paul's thought at this point, perhaps the assonance between Hebrew 'dar', *pearl*, and 'dal', short for 'deleth', *door* or *gate*, played a part in both their thinking.

It is thought that pearl is one of the hard-to-identify gemstones of the 'oracle of judgment'—the breastplate worn by Aaron and the high priests after him. If it's there, it is usually linked to the tribe of Zebulon.

(I think it's safe for us to ignore 'diamond', which is sometimes associated with Zebulon. The gemstones on the breastplate were engraved and, before the advent of diamond drills, this would have been an exceedingly tricky proposition. Quartz is harder to ignore as a possibility, but I'm inclined to think 'dar' and 'dal' would exert a hold on Paul's Hebrew mind—and besides, the marine nature of the pearl fits with the symbolism of the 'ships of Zebulon'. You might find quartz in grains of sand but you won't find it on a beach as a crystal big enough to engrave.)

Now, I admit the proposed mix for this floral and gemstone armour is a complex one comprised of both Hebrew and Greek imagery. However, I still think it's there and it's intentional, despite its subtlety: mustard flower and pearl.

One for 'faith' and the other for 'door'. That's what Paul planned, in my view.

Perhaps I'm influenced, however, by the way a very similar idea turned up in a completely unexpected context.

I had to extend my stride very quickly to avoid stepping on the most superb piece of polished pounamu I'd ever seen. A misty willow-green with pearl flecks and translucent sheen, it was an exquisite, flawless greenstone block embedded in concrete at the top of a wide set of stairs.

I was outside a restaurant on a wharf in the windy New Zealand capital, Wellington. The conference I was attending was about to open with a powhiri—a Māori welcome—and about 100 people were lined up, carefully following protocol as we waited for the traditional invitation to move onto the marae.

I'd just met up with Janette: she'd come from the South Island and I'd come over from the 'West Island'.[89] Six months previously we'd agreed to meet at this conference so we could pray specifically about the name and threshold covenants operating in her life.

Did either of us know what we were doing? That would be seriously over-estimating our giftings. We did, however, know we needed to deal with the stone, the watch and the seals.

It was the seals that were the problem. The knowledge of them can only be provided by God alone. Although Janette and I had had a commitment to pray for six months, we still needed a direct revelation regarding the seals covering the threshold.

As I awkwardly side-stepped this gorgeous piece of pounamu, several thoughts occurred to me: '*This is a stone in a threshold. Trampling on it doesn't seem like a good idea,*' and '*Jesus has obviously opened a seal,*' and '*God has to have arranged where I was standing in that crowd of 100 people. To move forward so that I would nearly step on the greenstone requires a precision formation. I've succeeded in noticing it but what is the message*?'

That was the problem in a nutshell: what was the message?

The Lord was talking in dark speech again.

And a translation was not readily at hand.

I talked to Janette about it. She suggested asking one of the Māori women who'd welcomed us onto the marae. So I sought out the kuia and asked her the meaning of the greenstone in the step.

'It's our taonga,' the kuia said. 'It is sacred. Normally it would be buried under the building but this is a commercial property. We lease it. If we had to move, then we would not want to lose the pounamu. So we put it in the step instead.'

Fortunately I'd lived in New Zealand for a time and I knew the word *taonga*: it's Māori for *treasure*. And more often than not when I'd encountered it, it had the connotation *treasure of the sea*.

Indeed the legend of the greenstone indicates it to be a treasure of the sea. There was a star in the constellation Orion which is called Poutini by the Māori people. Poutini became a fish and fell to Earth where it eventually turned into pounamu—greenstone. Having dropped into the ocean, it swam the ocean currents until it came to a cold resting place and heaved itself up as 'Te Wai Pounamu'—the South Island of New Zealand.

Now while this story of a galactic fish and a greenstone might seem odd, it has elements that are far from unique. For centuries greenstone, whether in Europe or Aotearoa, has been the most valued, treasured and sacred of stones.[90]

New Zealand's South Island—Te Wai Pounamu, *the place of greenstone*—was, according to the legend of Poutini, a sacred jewel which had risen from the sea. It was truly taonga.

Now what the kuia in the restaurant had told me indicated that greenstone was a sacred treasure at the heart of a home. Henry Clay Trumbull in his book *The Threshold Covenant* suggested that, before the threshold became the altar of a home in ancient times, the hearth was the sacred place.

The significance of a threshold is not so much as a doorway but as an altar. A place of sacred sacrifice.

The next day when I came to pray for Janette, I said to her: 'I think I've worked out what God was saying yesterday. It's a matter of translating the concept of 'treasure of the sea' across to another language and retaining its resonance of both a jewel and a sacred doorway. The only word I can think of that does this is 'pearl' which comes from the sea and is also the gate of heaven. I am therefore going to take it a step further and ask: "What does the name Margaret mean to you?"'

Janette took a deep breath. 'It's my middle name.'

It's probably no coincidence Satan had three attempts to lure Jesus into infidelity while He fasted in the wilderness. Jesus was on the threshold of His entry into ministry and Satan's efforts basically reflected the work of Talmai, Ahiman and Sheshai—doubt, still more doubt and an attempt to lay a false foundation.

Jesus famously countered every temptation by immediate recourse to the Word of God. Which He likened to, and distinguished from, bread.

Paul identifies the sword of the Spirit as the Word of God.

A sword that is spiritual food. A sword capable of nourishing those who use it while weakening those who oppose it. What a strange, otherworldly weapon.

I find it exceptionally cool that, in English, the word 'word' is sheathed within the word 'sword'. And that swords and words are intimately connected through the well-known proverb: *the pen is mightier than the sword.*

If we turn once more to the Hebrew language, we find an even more interesting wordplay than those which occur in English. There, the word for *scribe*, *writer* or *secretary*, 'caphar', rhymes with the word for *sapphire*, 'cappiyr'.

Surely it's no surprise there is another gemstone hiding in all this!

Although 'cappiyr' may not be our modern sapphire, it is definitely a gemstone of some kind. It may be a zircon—either deep purple hyacinth or rose-red jacinth.

In addition to the gemstone allusion, the threshold connection pops up again. The word for *scribe* is related to yet another concept within the environs of an entrance—the horizontal *sill* on which the *pivot* of an ancient door swung. In modern doorways with their slightly different construction, this would be equivalent to the *hinge*.

There is, however, another word in Hebrew for *hinge*: 'tsiyr'. The same word means *ambassador*. As an ambassador joins one country to another, so a hinge joins a door and a wall. It should be no surprise 'tsiyr' is related to the word for *stress*. We can be sure Paul was thinking of this because he finishes up his description of God's armour by requesting prayer for himself, an ambassador in chains.

Whenever we take up the sword of the Spirit, we are as ambassadors joining heaven and earth. The complexity and richness of allusion here is almost breathtaking. *God's Panoply* discusses how Psalm 85 reveals heaven and earth meeting in the kiss of peace, righteousness, truth and faithful mercy. These elements too are encoded in Paul's description of the armour.

Still we're far from finished. We have yet to identify the flower hidden in the sword. Simplicity itself: it's the manna ash. Manna is the 'bread of heaven' provided by God in the wilderness. Nutritious edible flakes that floated in on the wind,[91] it was a well-recognised symbol of the Word of God. For forty years, manna appeared almost daily during the desert wanderings of the Israelites. It only stopped when they finally camped inside the Promised Land.

So Paul was not just talking about the Word of God as essential to our armorial gear. Like the other items in the divine armour, it's far more than it seems at a superficial glance. The sword of the Spirit is:

- an ambassador's pen
- a manna ash blossom
- a sapphire (or jacinth) encrusted sword
- a hinge for door-opening and closing

How breathtaking is this?

As I've struggled to identify which of the twelve gemstones on the high priest's breastplate Paul excluded from the armour of God—*and why*—I was troubled that, by having to include alabaster and pearl, things got worse and not better.

Then I found this: *'I proceeded and saw a place which burns day and night, where there are seven mountains of magnificent stones, three towards the east, and three towards the south. And as for those towards the east, one was of coloured stone, and one of pearl, and one of jacinth, and those towards the south of red stone. But the middle one reached to heaven like the throne of God, of alabaster, and the summit of the throne was of sapphire.'* (1 Enoch 18:6–8, translated by RH Charles)

This excerpt is from the book of Enoch, which was wildly popular in first-century Galilee and quoted in the writings of the apostles. It is said it's impossible to understand the New Testament without examining the Book of Enoch. Jude's epistle famously acknowledges its indebtedness to it and appears to quote 1 Enoch 1:9.

The well-known phrase 'King of kings and Lord of lords' used several times in the New Testament does not occur in the Old, but first appears in the Book of Enoch.

Some mysterious references in 1 Peter 3 about the spirits in prison may also come from the Book of Enoch—in fact, from the incident occurring right after Enoch sees the seven gemstone mountains. Only six of those jewelled heights are actually described: coloured stone, pearl, jacinth, red stone, alabaster, sapphire.

Now it's said 'jacinth' should more correctly be rendered *stone of healing* but nevertheless the list gives me hope I am on the right track in identifying the jewels of the armour of God.

Although we may think it strange the list comes from outside the established biblical canon, the value of the Book of Enoch is demonstrated by the fact it is quoted within Scripture.

The penultimate item of armour in our roundup is the Belt of Truth.

The 'baltus', *belt*, of a first century Roman soldier was often a baldric which crossed the body diagonally. Instead of just circling the waist, we should picture it as also passing over the shoulder. Containing a sword sheath, it was often carved or encrusted with jewels and precious metals. An identity statement, the baltus was practical but also served as a soldier's personal adornment. They were so valuable that looters often went to battlefields to strip the dead of these 'spoils of war'.

So when Paul wrote of the Belt of Truth, I'm inclined to think he meant the 'baltus' which enabled a warrior of God to keep the sword of the Spirit, the Word of God, close to his heart. Its position on the shoulder would have signalled, at least to the Hebrew mind, truth's significance as resting on the seat of authority. When a Jewish father wanted to confer authority on his son, he would place a set of keys on his shoulder. Hence the famous line from Isaiah, sung resoundingly in Handel's *Messiah*: '*and the government shall be upon His shoulder.*'

Government here implies the keys of authority. As we noted previously, the name Cleopatra may mean *keys of the fatherland*. Its male equivalent is Cleopas.

The disciple Cleopas is mentioned only once in Scripture—when he walks with a friend to Emmaus and encounters Jesus on the way. Initially failing to recognise Him, they discuss the death of the man they had hoped was the Messiah. And in the course of the conversation, Jesus hands them the keys to understanding how He fulfilled all the prophecies spoken of Him down the ages.

To me, it's obvious Cleopas was immensely influential in the early church—simply because he was one of only two people who had received these keys. The authority he had to interpret prophecy came directly from Jesus Himself.

Authority, for a Christian, should also be none other than the Word of God—as what we stand on, what we stand under and what we stand for. However, in today's world the authority of Scripture seems as relativistic as truth was in the first century.

Jesus clearly wanted to re-establish truth and integrity as an indivisible unit. He commanded his disciples not to take oaths but to let their 'yes' be yes and their 'no' be no. Given that even Paul took oaths,[92] Jesus seems to have been talking about truth, not oaths per se. A whole system of rules had been developed by the scribes and Pharisees around the taking of oaths so that the teaching in the Law of Moses could be preserved while still practising lying and deception! As Andrew Reid says, 'these systems of oath-taking actually fostered lying, not truth-telling.'[93]

While we tend to think of truth as a solid bulwark, there's also a sense in which it is very fragile. So perhaps it's appropriate that the flower I believe is hidden behind a veil of allusion here is one of the most delicate of all: the anemone or windflower.

The vivid red anemone was a wildflower in Israel and was said in Canaanite mystery religion to signify the blood of Adonis whose name means *lord*. Now, as it happens, *blood* in Greek is also *spirit*. *Wind* and *spirit* are cognates in many languages, so perhaps we are meant to recall Jesus' words that true worshippers would approach the Father in spirit and truth. Or is it blood and truth?

Now I don't want to add too much fuel to the unquenchable theological mine-fire over what Jesus meant when He said, *'This is the new covenant in My blood ...'* by noting He might have said, *' ... in My spirit ...'*

I simply want to note, as I did previously in *God's Panoply*, that the Greek gospels are already translations and that the cultural gap between Hebrew and Greek is vast. Yet Paul not only tried to bridge it, he was able to play poetically and prophetically with language. The last three syllables of the Greek word, anemone—*windflower*—are essentially the Hebrew word 'enumah', *firm, faithful, trust.* 'Enumah' is derived from "'aman', often translated *truth.*[94]

It's a lovely pun that spans two languages. 'Enumah' is the word used in Paul's quote from Habukkuk—'*The just shall live by faith* ('enumah')'—which revolutionised the Christian world during the Protestant Reformation.

I believe that Paul was, in all this, again alluding to Ephesian Artemis, his sights on her alternate guise as the hell-goddess Hekate.

Hekate was said to hold the keys to the gates of Hades and to guard crossroads. Paul, with incredible subtlety, directed the Ephesian readers to the words of Jesus when He undertook a name covenant with Peter at Caesarea Phillipi in the territory which once belonged to the key-wielder, Cleopatra. Paul's message is that hell is not going to prevail: The Way, the Truth and the Life is.

To sum up, death is conquered and its authority smashed. Paul reminds us so in this simple phrase, 'belt of truth', which evokes:

- a jewelled belt of faithfulness, trust and truth
- keys and seat of authority in heavenly places
- a carved statement of identity in Christ
- a wild anemone reminding us our cover is the blood of Jesus

This brings us to the last weapon in the Armour of God. Many commentators miss this seventh item, even though the rest are pretty much useless without it. Let's return for a moment to Paul's inspiration for 'shoes of the gospel of peace', Isaiah 52:7—*How beautiful upon the mountains are the feet of the messenger who announces peace, who brings good news.*

The last item in the arsenal of God alludes to the very next verse, Isaiah 52:8—*Listen! Your watchmen lift up their voices; together they shout for joy. When the Lord returns to Zion, they will see it with their own eyes.*

Yes, it's about *watching*. More precisely it's about watchful prayer. About being alert and being ready to break into petition and praise at a moment's notice. Again we should be reminded of that wonderful exchange between God and Jeremiah.

'What do you see?'

'An almond tree.'

'You're right! I'm watching over My word to activate My promises.'

The almond blossom, the first to 'wake up' in spring, the symbol of the alert watcher, the emblem of promise-yet-to-be-fulfilled, is the seventh and last flower hidden in the Armour of God.

My guess for a gemstone—and I stress it's a guess—is amethyst. In Greek, *preventer of drunkenness*. In Hebrew, *dreamstone*. Because we need to awaken, activate the promises of God and use the dreams He has given us in an appropriate fashion: whether those dreams be visionary aspirations about the calling on our lives or even nightmare warnings of imminent spiritual attack.[95]

Pray at all times in the Spirit with all manner of prayer and entreaty. To that end, keep alert and watch with strong purpose and perseverance, interceding on behalf of all the saints.

(Ephesians 6:18 AMP)

Here again are subtle allusions:

- almond blossom, the herald of spring
- amethyst to remind us to be sober and act on our dreams
- watchers who turn back the battle at the gates
- petitioning ambassadors who represent others before God

Did you ever imagine all this pageantry was encoded in the 101 Greek words describing the Armour of God?

And this is not the end of it. In *God's Panoply*, I point out the mathematics of the sequence is about sevenfold covenant. I also point out the choice of weaponry—truth, mercy, righteousness and peace—indicates the kiss of heaven and earth mentioned in Psalm 85:10–11.

I'm vastly suspicious geographical references are here too. But I'm not entirely sure.[96] If there are, then surely they're about healing the land.

This beautiful, jewelled, sweet-smelling armour is not meant for ourselves alone. It is given to us so we can defend others. As watchmen, we are to praise God. And because God inhabits the praises of His people, draw His presence and His glory to dwell with us.

When Moses asked to see God's glory, God permitted him a glimpse of His back. Announcing His identity, He said: *The Lord! The Lord! A God merciful and gracious, slow to anger and abundant in lovingkindness and truth. Keeping mercy and lovingkindness for thousands, forgiving iniquity and transgressions and sin. But who will by no means clear the guilty.*

Mercy, truth, justice and peace. Here they are again—as in Psalm 85.

The kiss of God is still the best way to don His armour.

6

Over the Threshold

LET ME BEGIN WITH a warning. The threshold is unspeakably dangerous. Presume nothing. Put your armour on. Lift your face for the kiss of God.[97]

God may sovereignly deal, in an instant, with the various dark covenants and stumbling blocks over your life. However, in my experience, He desires most people to work out the issues in fear and trembling.

There appear to be certain non-negotiable preparations beforehand. You must have renounced:

- your false refuge and also have passed His subsequent test for you—that is, when disappointment struck again, you ran to Him and didn't lick your wounds in your old way
- your covenant with death and have received a sign from God it has been annulled—this sign is something *extremely* unusual in the natural world

These two steps, found in Isaiah 28:15, are necessary precursors to dealing with a threshold covenant. The threshold covenant itself is mentioned in Isaiah 28:16. If you do not know how to go about these steps, carefully read *God's Poetry* and *God's Panoply* in this series.

Do not be in haste.

If you've already completed the two steps above, then proceed as follows. This is a general strategy, not a set of rules. I've set out what I believe is the best order but the Holy Spirit may suggest otherwise for you.

Pray that God will cause you to remember everything necessary; pray your memories are not snatched away and that, if fearful recollections surface, you will not be paralysed but deal with them as an alert watchman would: sound the alarm and ask Jesus for help.

As suggested in *God's Poetry*, deal with your name covenant by asking Jesus (it's worth specifying 'of Nazareth') to intervene for you. Ask Him to step into your name and make it a gate of praise.

The reason a threshold covenant is complicated is the threefold guard:

- the stone
- the watch
- the seal

Each is complex in its own right and may take significant time to work through. Why should we expect instant solutions when, for both the patriarchs and for Jesus Himself, a natural 'time of life' was involved? In my experience this process takes, *at minimum*, about fourteen months.

First, tackle the watch over the threshold. The threshold guardians comprise the watch: the constrictor and waster—Python and Rachab.

Ask God (it is worth specifying Abba, the Father of Jesus of Nazareth here) for His matchless mercy and for the covering of the blood of Jesus as you petition Him to install the cherubim on your own personal threshold. If the idea of installing the cherubim on your threshold doesn't scare you witless, you have not understood the gravity of what you are asking and it's advisable not to do it. If you do not have reverential respect for God at this point, you need to repent of presumption and wait until God says you are ready.

The purpose of asking the cherubim onto your threshold is so they can fight for you. It is not your business to bind Python or Rachab. Such an attempt may actually provide legal grounds for a counter-attack. Simply keep out of the way of the cherubim and keep your eyes fixed on God and on building a gateway of praise to Him.

Wait until there is evidence the cherubim have had the victory over the spirits of constriction and wasting and that you have passed over the threshold. This evidence may be some time in coming—weeks, even months—and there may be no visible sign or sense of anything very much different. The first evidence may be that you experience backlash in situations at work or at home: Leviathan has arrived and is making itself known.

As I've frankly admitted, I don't know much about the activity of Leviathan. It's not a spirit I have encountered to any great degree,[98] though I am well acquainted with its servants, the spirits of wasting and silence. I believe Leviathan only has legal grounds to attack those who maintain an attitude of disrespect for any aspect of God's creation (including fallen spirits themselves). Therefore, it's wise to renounce and repent of any specific activity that could fall into this category either on your own part or your ancestors. Also ask God's forgiveness for abusing His creation and for not simply asking Him to rebuke the cosmic powers involved. Fasting may be necessary: Jesus' remark in Mark 9:29 about spirits that can only be ousted by prayer and fasting comes, significantly perhaps, immediately after the threshold event of the Transfiguration.

Second, the stone and the seals have to be dealt with. You can prepare for this while waiting for the cherubim to complete their work. Your threshold stone has something written on it. You need to find out what that is. And it's fairly easy. Simply finish the following sentence with the very first thought that comes to mind: *If ever I were to come into my destiny, then ...*

There are a number of possible inscriptions for threshold stones in Scripture[99] but my guess is, what's written on yours isn't one of them. Now there's no point at all in dealing with this unless you've found the seals over your tomb.

Here's where it all comes apart for those of us who really want a formula to 'fix' threshold covenants. A seal is basically a demonic failsafe; if the spirits of constriction, wasting and backlash as well as the vow-activating inscription on your threshold stone are deactivated, the curses of the seals are designed to take you down anyway.

There's usually more than one seal and they self-trigger; in the event the first is found and defused through prayer, the second goes into automatic countdown. So it's necessary to find out how many seals there are and deal with *all of them at once*. There can be as many as seven seals. The only person able to open them is Jesus.

Imagine this: you've got a box that will explode unless you use just the right key. But the right key is already locked inside the box.

That's what a seal is like. You can't open the box without the key and you can't get the key unless you can open the box. Your only hope is for Jesus to reach in and get it. So you have to wait on Him. And it may take a while, especially if more than one seal is involved.[100]

If, by this stage, you're still working alone on this problem, stop. Your general, not specific, calling is to the Body of Christ and, if you're still grimly holding to your individuality, you're not ready to cross the threshold. You should be working with at least one prayer partner.

The seals over thresholds are usually weird and, in my experience, connected in an unexpected symbolic way to your name. They are like the geis described in Irish legend: a binding woven into a name that, if broken, is meant to bring about your destruction.

Here are some seals I have encountered just to indicate how odd they can be: the letter 'e', fire and water, pearl, a silver hand, a fox, a basket.

How to proceed with a prayer partner:

- Once all the seals are identified by the Holy Spirit, ask Jesus to remove them. Name the seals and specifically renounce any allegiance on the part of your ancestors to any spirit empowering the seals and renounce your own complicity in keeping the seals intact through fear or lack of faith.
- Ask the Holy Spirit as your paraclete to take the sword of the Word of God and cut any connection between the seals and your name.
- Renounce, repent and seek forgiveness for whatever faulty inscription is on your threshold stone. Your threshold stone *may* also be a family foundation stone passed down from your ancestors, so vows may be involved.
- Dismantle the vows through the power of the Cross and ask

God for the authority to dismiss any unholy spirits attached to those vows.

- Dismiss them with respect and courtesy and ask God to send His angels to escort them to the place He has reserved for them at this time. Do not assume where that place is.
- Repent of your failure to believe that Jesus is the one-and-only, all-sufficient sacrifice needed to come into your destiny. If you have actually been a threshold sacrifice yourself, you need to seek forgiveness for empowering others to cross the threshold (regardless of whether that was your intention or not) and for usurping the place of Christ in the threshold covenant. If you feel like you are staked to the threshold, you should ask Jesus to remove gently the nail that holds your spirit there and bind up your broken heart. This particular step can come at any time in the process, even right at the beginning, before dealing with the threshold guardians. But it is good to re-affirm it now.
- Ask Jesus to take up the threshold stone of your life, deal with it as He chooses, and replace it with Himself as cornerstone.
- Ask God to write a Scripture verse with His finger on your new cornerstone and to tell you what it is.
- Ask the Holy Spirit to tell you what you've overlooked and to seal Christ's work of redemption in you.

What are you, O great mountain? ... you will become a plain. And he will bring forth the top stone with shouts of, 'Grace, grace to it!'

Zechariah 4:7 NAS

You may discover in this process that your healing and the healing of your land (or inheritance) are intimately tied together.[101] Isaiah 27:2 tells us to sing to our inheritance. Remind it that it belongs to God, not Leviathan.

Then rest in the Lord. The time it takes before you have a new sense of destiny should be around nine months. Yes, it's like birth. There are many reasons this process can miscarry. If it does, go to God, ask Him why and expect an answer. If you don't get an answer, ask Him what blockage is stopping it.

There are almost certainly surprises in store: you are probably not who you think you are and your destiny almost certainly not what you expected it to be.

It's far, far better.

7

The Courts of the King

When I was a teenager, I had a recurring nightmare. I would be sitting on a beach under some palm trees, watching the waves crashing onto the shore. Suddenly I'd notice there were strange shadows darting over the waves—or was it *within* them? Castles and spires, ruined battlements and towering trees seemed caught in the ebb and flow of the surf.

I'd look up and begin to suspect the palm trees were signalling to the shadows.

An undefined menace would gain solidity within the water.

I'd turn and run.

I would find myself sprinting along a golden thread, as thin as a strand of hair. The golden thread led into a dark vaulted place and glowed softly, showing the way. I'd hear a thunderous footfall. A monstrous tree had stepped out of the waves behind me.

Curiously I was always able to maintain my balance on the incredibly thin thread. As I hurried along, it shimmered, twisting back and forward, under and over, up, down and through the high vaulted place.

Looking back on the dream as an adult, I realise the golden thread was a vast Celtic knot leading through time and space. But back then I didn't recognise its shape. I only knew I had to follow the thread and not try to jump across to another part of it. I had that preternatural knowledge existing in dreams that I could only keep ahead of the malevolent tree if I didn't try to second-guess its moves.

A platform would appear in front of me. It floated in some high and lonely place, beside the glowing thread. A bunch of wildflowers was on it. There were eight or nine of them wrapped in tissue paper, each perfect, each a different colour and variety.

I'd step onto the platform. The flowers were mine, but I was hesitant to pick them up. I was even more hesitant to leave them. They would be destroyed by the monstrous tree: it was like leaving part of myself behind even to contemplate going without them. However, if I took them, I'd be unable to balance on the golden thread. Sooner, rather than later, I would fall.

Then I'd hear a Voice. *'Don't worry about it. They will be on your pillow when you wake up.'*

With only the tiniest of backward glances, I'd leave them behind and set off again along the glowing thread. But the first thing I always did when I woke from this nightmare was look for the wildflowers on my pillow.

They were never there.

I first told this story in *God's Poetry*, interpreting the wildflowers (a recurring element across a wide variety of nightmares) as a motif referring to my name. I realise now they were also emblematic of armour.

Time after time, I left behind the armour God had graced me with—but was reassured by His promise it would be ready for me when I woke up. Like Sleeping Beauty, I needed a kiss to wake me from my spiritual sleep. But the kiss of Jesus is also His way of arming us with Himself: He is our salvation, He is our breastplate, He is our peace, He is the Word, He is our truth and our faith.

Those of us who are still subject to constriction, wasting or backlash haven't crossed the threshold.

Many of us are like Kevin, whom I mentioned way back in the prologue, baulking at the last moment. We've flunked every test and we've become terrified of passing. Hope deferred has made our hearts sick.

I used to sit beside Kevin and talk him through the difficult problems. God goes one better. He'll actually give us the answers!

He wants us to know why we can't cross the threshold. He wants to remove the blocks.

Because all of His wondrous pageantry—the armour, the kiss, the wildflowers, the gemstones, the mathematics and the covenant—is about lifting us, as His bride, over His threshold into the courts of heaven.

And, once there, for goodness and mercy to follow us all the days of our lives.

For our destiny to greet us, our calling to take us by the hand.

For Him to sing with joy over us.

Forever.

Endnotes

1 According to the on-line news service *Eureka Street*: 'Only in a society practising sexual idolatry as the basis of identity could such confusion arise. As the gay sexologist Foucault said: "Sexuality has replaced the soul." The over-heated rhetoric of denying people their humanity because of inability to fully express their sexuality insults millions of celibates. [Justice Michael] Kirby claims that the source of the churches' "terrible pickle over human sexuality" is "the age old problem of the text. And the human disinclination in the face of *new* knowledge, to adjust to the necessities of *new* thinking." This almost automatic rejection of the old or traditional contradicts Kirby's support of the monarchy, or Anglican liturgy, or much law. It denies what Chesterton calls *'the democracy of the dead'.* The vast and panoramic past has a right to vote, against the dictatorial parochialism and diminished perspective of the present.'

2 This raises difficult questions about dementia. Is identity simply to do with memory? (I certainly hasten to clarify that, by using the Jewish story of the angel at the gates of heaven, I don't want to suggest that is all it is.)

3 In *God's Poetry: The Identity and Destiny Encoded in Your Name* I assert that, while traditionally James is derived from Jacob, *usurper, deceiver, foot-grasper,* it makes more sense for it to come from 'jamin', *right hand,* as in Benjamin, *son of my right hand.*

4 There are at least 68 beginnings in the first four chapters alone according to Kameel Majdali in *Understanding Genesis.*

5 Note the Hebrew pun on 'man', *adam* and 'ground', *adamah.*

6 Puzzled that 'shem' doesn't look like 'shim' or 'sham'? Hebrew has no vowels but English includes vowels to help us say the words.

7 http://www.torah.org/features/par-kids/names.html

8 'In the ancient world, a name was a person's identity. It was far more than a distinguishing label or an indicator of family heritage. A person's name said something about who the person was in character or nature. Most babies in Bible times were not named until the eighth day after their birth... In addition, it was a custom in Bible times that mothers spent hours singing and talking to their unborn children, bonding with them in a deep emotional and spiritual way. This bonding gave mothers special insight into the personalities and destinies of the babies in their wombs.' (Michael Youssef, *Discover the Power of One: make your life count*)

9 Josephus, the Jewish historian, also mentions *elicio.* Carried out at the instigation of King Alexander Jannaeus, one of the Maccabees, a god of Edom was summoned to Jerusalem. The examples given in this section are from R Graves, *The White Goddess – a historical grammar of poetic myth*, Farrar, Strauss and Giroux, New York, 1999.

10 The idea of the power of a name along with the notion that destiny is entwined with it is common in classical and modern fantasy. A chapter on this appears in

God's Poetry: The Identity and Destiny Encoded in Your Name. Largely, however, the idea has disappeared from western consciousness. I believe fantasy is the last great outpost of the notion of the power of naming in this century. Nevertheless, as children, before we are seduced into modern scientific rationalism, we instinctively know of the power of naming. Gordon Dalbey in *No Small Snakes: A Journey into Spiritual Warfare* notes that little children intuitively grasp the concept of naming and its power. They may lisp and stutter most of the time but certain six-syllable names roll off their tongues with ease. He points out a small boy is powerless amongst adult giants. The ones who control him are the ones who must meet his needs. Not only do they not bow to his wants, they try to mould his behaviour. Here is a situation intrinsically fearful—and, into it, steps a giant who dwarfs even these huge adults. The dinosaur. Gigantic, powerful, destructive, uncontrollable. Better still: real. Best of all: extinct. 'To know promises the ability to master. And so the little boy reads, he studies, he learns, and, like Adam, he names—especially six-syllable species. ...*Violà!* Mastery over the fear. I can control this awesome power. In my hands, in my vocabulary, in the grip of my imagination, the beast is subdued.' It is no coincidence this insight comes from a man who had trouble with his name. After being baffled for years by the fact people mistakenly called him 'Roger', he examined the possibility they intuitively discerned the name God had given him.

11 Luke 8:44; these tassels on the prayer shawl are known in Hebrew as *tzitzit.*

12 He was actually a twin—fraternal, according to tradition—his sister's name allegedly being Lysia. However, I believe 'Didymus' (which actually does mean *twin*) may be more of a nickname than a translation.

13 Sometimes, because of the qualifier 'many', it's given as *rich farmer.* The relationship between Ptolemy and Talmai is tricky. Talmay (Talmai), meaning *furrowed* and coming from 'telem', *furrow, to accumulate (wealth)* starts with the Hebrew letter tav. It may be related to Talmon, *oppressor* from 'telem', *oppression* or *break up violently* but this is not entirely certain as it starts with teth, not tav. Clearly, however, 'telem' (with a teth) is the root of Ptolemy, *aggressive, war-like,* and thus of Bartholemew. If Thomas really is related to Bartholemew, then it also resonates with *oppression* and *aggression*, again relating Thomas to Talmai, son of Anak.

14 And since it is faith that saves, not any inherent goodness or good works of our own, perhaps this incident is also a subtle commentary on another possible meaning of Tom. (Not so much of Thomas, but the nickname Tom.) Tom sounds far too much like Hebrew for *good, perfect* and *right hand,* so the significance of faith in this story should probably not be underestimated.

15 The gaps in Franklin's work are, I think, due to lack of experience. He's obviously had some close-quarter engagement but not for an extended period. I lack similar close-quarter engagement with Leviathan over a long period of time which, I believe, also produces gaps in my commentary on it.

16 http://www.fbbc.com/messages/farm_plow.htm

17 I first heard a curious story about Elimelekh and Zusia in Charles Osborne's symphonic suite, *Souls on Fire.* During their travels they came to a village

outside of Cracow where they intended to stay. However, they felt strangely compelled to leave. The name of the village? Oswieçim is its Polish name. However during the Nazi occupation of World War II, it received a German name. It retained that name after the end of the war, even when other towns reverted to their original Polish. We know it as Auschwitz.

18 Often it's the day before, as well. This is so common it's impossible to overstate its importance. For a long course (such as a university course), the threshold moment might occur in the last few weeks. It's surprising how many people give up just before the end or alternatively sabotage themselves with an 'out of character' action such as participating in minor criminal activity.

19 Michael Jensen in *Pieces of Eternity* writes about the creation of a synthetic genetic code and quotes biological engineer Drew Endy of Stanford University: 'It's not genesis... The correct word is *poesis*, human construction. We can now go from information and get a reproducing organism.' Thus Endy uses the base of the word *poetry* to describe what makes a human life.

20 '"Delicacies" were so called because the food has been offered first to the idols of the... pagan gods. The pagan peoples of the ancient world ate the leftovers of foods sacrificed to their gods as a means of identifying with the gods.' (Michael Youssef, *Discover the Power of One: make your life count.*)

21 It's difficult to tell how long Terah delayed in Haran—it could have been five years or five decades. We know Abram was 75 when he left Haran for Canaan and that, as Abraham, he died 100 years later. It's difficult to reconcile the account in Genesis with what Stephen says in Acts 7. Stephen says Abram lived in Haran until Terah died. However, the account in Genesis appears to say that Terah continued to live in Haran for 70 years after Abram left. Obviously a translation issue. However, going back to the time Abram actually dwelt in Haran: assuming the family left Ur when Abram was 25 and Sarai 15, that would make a 50 year delay. But if they left when Abram was 70 and Sarai 60, it would only be 5 years. The very fact that time is taken to mention it does, however, suggest that the time in Haran was considerable.

22 This is one of the most wonderful aspects of all creation in my view. It's also one of the most overlooked. Starlight, because *it is light*, travels through space at the speed *of light*. That might seem self-evident but it has remarkable implications. According to Einstein's Theory of Relativity, the faster an object goes then the slower time appears to go, according to an observer outside its 'frame of reference'. For any object travelling at the speed of light, no time appears to pass. Sunlight appears to us to take eight minutes to travel from the sun to the earth but, if we could quiz a light photon on how long it took, it would say it had left a bare instant ago. Light from Proxima Centauri, the closest star system, seems to astronomers to take 4.3 years. But, if we could ask the light itself, it would say it had just left, the merest fraction of a second ago. Time and eternity are so intertwined it's possible for us to go out under the night sky and, like Abraham, experience light falling on us that comes from the very dawn of creation. Mind-blowing as this next thought is, it's true: we can actually join with the singing of the morning stars, at the beginning of time,

in their very first hymn of praise to God. Relativity has stunning consequences. It means that, in Job 38:7, when God questions Job about where he was when the morning stars first shouted for joy on seeing heaven and earth spring into being, the answer is mysterious and mind-bending: *'right here, right now'*. And the most thrilling aspect is that, if God were to ask us the same question, that answer would be true for us too! (*The Singing Silence*, Anne Hamilton) The Bible implicitly and explicitly refers to relativity in relation to time. The relevant transformation factor appears in 2 Peter 3:8, bypassing all of Einstein's work to give us a straight-forward multiplication. Anyone trying to establish the age of the earth should take relativity into account. Because six thousand years in one 'frame of reference' transforms to roughly 4.4 billion years in the other. (Roughly, because I'm estimating 12 hours in a day since the Greek word Peter uses refers to the period of daylight, rather than 24-hour day.) In this, the Bible confirms *both* sides of the argument in the young and old earth debate! You don't need a degree in physics to check this. Just turn 6000 years into the equivalent number of days, multiply by 2 because strictly it's 'daylight hours' rather than 'days' and then multiply by 1000. *Violà!* (This doesn't automatically support evolution, by the way.)

23 'If you were lost in the desert (back in ancient times), the children of Israel would have been required by the law of hospitality to satisfy your need for food, water, protection from an enemy, and shade from the blistering sun. It worked like this: first you had to find out the chief shepherd's name. Then you would take hold of the cord on his tent and cry out for help. When you did that, the law of hospitality required him to take you into the safety of his tent. Indeed, that same law said he had to protect you with his very life.' (Bob Gass, *The Word for Today*)

24 Did Rahab also marry Joshua? Although some commentators suggest it was another woman with the same name, I think it's not unlikely to be Rahab of Jericho. (Why mention it otherwise?) The essential nature of covenant is oneness. That is what distinguishes it from a contract. *There is neither Jew nor Greek, there is neither slave nor free man, there is neither male nor female; for you are all one in Christ Jesus.* (Galatians 3:28 NAS)

25 There's an illuminating discussion on the names Abram and Abraham at the *Abarim Publications* website worth checking. Although the 'rhm' overlap referring to covenant-cutting is noted there, it is considered too 'poetic' to be likely. However, poetry is precisely why I think it is.

26 Actually three names sprang to mind, the third being 'Mabon'. But since Mabon is occasionally conflated with Taliesin, and moreover, it didn't rhyme with Alison, I let it go immediately.

27 It would be perilous to assume, from this example, the name Alison actually derives in an etymological sense from Taliesin. For this particular Alison, it was prophetic sense. God isn't limited to etymology or linguistic science when it comes to the destiny encoded in our names. He is a poet (Ephesians 2:10). He uses all the wonder of poetry—head rhyme, tail rhyme, assonance, anagrams, cognates—when designing a future and a hope for each one of us. Thus, for other Alisons, it will be different. For those of a Spanish heritage, *alder* might be the mythic

background; for those of a Central European background, it might be *fox*.

28 I'm assuming that you, as a reader, are a Christian.

29 My translation.

30 See *God's Poetry: The Identity and Destiny Encoded in Your Name* for further detail on these names.

31 A 'shaliach' is a messenger/ambassador invested with plenipotentiary powers. This means the messenger is to be accorded the same status as the sender of the message, treated in the same way and seen effectively as the sender himself. Thus a shaliach sent on behalf of a king *is*, in a real sense, the king. Hence why so many angels mentioned in Scripture are messengers one second and God the next. Because they have been sent by God with plenipotentiary status, their actions are God's actions.

32 Personally I am not convinced this is the origin of the H. It could be from 'heyeh' or 'ehyeh' (one of the several transliterations for the name of God, given to Moses at the Burning Bush.) 'Yahweh' is a step removed from this name.

33 Israel is the name given to Jacob after his fight with the Angel of God (Genesis 32:28).

The meaning of the name Israel is not clear, although it is most likely a compound of the verb 'sara' and the noun 'el'. The meaning of 'sara' is uncertain and explained in many ways, chiefly because it is limited to contexts which discuss the struggle of Jacob with the Angel of the Lord. It may be related to 'misra', a unique word probably meaning *rule* or *dominion*, used in Isaiah 8:6, '...and the *government* is on His shoulder.' Nobody knows what the root of this word is but linguists have related it to Israel. Another possibility is that Israel uses the verb 'sarar', meaning *to rule, reign, act as prince*. 'Sar' means *prince*, and 'Sarah', *princess*, is the name of Jacob's grandmother. Although we cannot say with certainty what the name Israel means, we can note the circumstances in which it was given. The story makes it seem like God was not able to defeat Jacob. Since God does not lack the power to triumph over any human, it must be concluded that the destruction of Jacob would go against the very nature of God. Perhaps the name Israel denotes God's continuous effort to keep Jacob going, even though Jacob continues to fight God.
http://www.abarim-publications.com/Meaning/Israel.html

34 Y Eckstein, 'By the Light of the Moon', *Holy Land Moments Daily Devotional*, 19 February 2014. Eckstein goes on to explain that the women were rewarded for this attitude with a monthly holiday. Every new moon there is a mini-holiday exclusively for the women.

35 *God's Panoply: The Armour of God and the Kiss of Heaven* gives a fuller explanation of the consequences of this.

36 K Bailey, *Poet and Peasant: A Literary-Cultural Approach to the Parables in Luke.*

37 Here's just a dozen involving angels guarding both the place and the time of change. There are many more:

- The ultimate threshold moment—the new beginning when Death itself is defeated: Jesus is raised from the dead. When Mary is standing outside the tomb, having come to anoint His body with spices, she sees two angels inside. (John 20:11-12)

- Jesus ascends to heaven, forty days after His resurrection. Two angels appear and ask the disciples why they're staring at a blank sky. (Acts 1:10)
- Angel choirs announce Jesus' birth.
- When He began his ministry, angels ministered to Him after He had spent forty days in the desert, being tempted by Satan.
- Mary was visited by an angel, announcing she was chosen to bear God's Son. So, too, the husband of her cousin Elizabeth encountered an angel who told him his wife was to have a son in her old age.
- Jacob left his father-in-law Laban and headed home to reconcile with the brother he cheated decades earlier. On the way, he met the angels of God. '*When Jacob saw them, he said, "This is the camp of God!" So he named that place Mahanaim.*' (Genesis 32:2 NIV) Later that night he wrestled with one of them by the ford of Jabbok. As dawn broke he refused to let the angel go until he received a blessing, he got a new name: Israel, *prince of God* or *who struggles with God*. This story is full of threshold moments: a final leaving, crossing a ford, the breaking of dawn, the meeting with his brother, a new beginning, a new name.
- Abraham gave hospitality—including undertaking a threshold covenant—to two angels on their way to Sodom. God, who was with them, announced that Sarah would soon give birth to a son to be named Isaac, the child of the promise.
- Lot gave hospitality to two angels within Sodom, undertaking a threshold covenant with them. Hence his obligation to defend them (even to the point of offering his own daughters to the debauchers) and hence also their reciprocal defence of him, not just in blinding the attackers but in leading his family out of the city to safety. The angels would have rescued Lot anyway, even if he had not committed to the threshold covenant with them: they had been part of the threshold covenant with Abraham and were thus obligated to protect Abraham's family, which included his nephew Lot.
- Joshua encounters the angelic Commander of the army of the Lord as he prepares for his first battle in the Promised Land.
- David goes to the threshing floor of Ornan the Jebusite where a destroying angel has halted, sword stretched over Jerusalem. He buys the threshing floor as a site for the building of the Temple. (1 Chronicles 21)
- Gideon is threshing wheat, hidden in a winepress, when an angel appears to him and announces he is the one chosen to free Israel from the oppression of the Midianites. (Judges 6:11)
- The first Passover.

38 The kangaroo would have been better but it wasn't really an option at the time. Frogs and toads are another possibility but they aren't exactly kosher.

39 See *God's Poetry: The Identity and Destiny Encoded in Your Name* for dozens of examples, both Biblical and contemporary. One I'd like to take the opportunity to add here is Michal, daughter of Saul. Ordinary etymology reveals her name is like Michael and means 'who is like the Lord?' It gives us no clue as to why it would be recorded she never had children. Nor does it offer hints why the biggest single glimpse we get into her life is where she is looking out the window, sees David dancing before the Ark of the Lord and despises him. Obviously the

chronicler wants us to see the connection between this incident and her lack of children. Most people read into it a punishment of God. In fact, that's not there at all. What the story reveals is that Michal hated herself. Her name is a simple poetic assonance with 'machowl', *dance* or *dancing*. In rejecting David's offering of dance to the Lord, she rejects her own name, calling and identity. This indicates one of the most important aspects of names: they are not determinants of unavoidable fate. Every name encodes a choice: we can decide to experience the fullness of our calling and accept God's invitation into destiny, or we can turn our backs on it. Choose or refuse: it's entirely up to us. I've known several women who truly hated their names and all had trouble conceiving.

40 Whether Abraham's father was still alive and back in Haran at this time is unclear. But if he were alive, then for a man like Abraham with the obvious family loyalty he had, this was clearly an issue. The commandment about honouring your parents was still some centuries away but it was already part of the culture—perhaps, it could be argued, it's a natural law. Jewish rabbinical commentary has attempted some truly creative explanations to get around this issue, but it does so by trying to make Abraham an exception to all the rules: honouring his father in the breach, rather than the observance. Quite frankly, it doesn't wash: Abraham's action twenty-four years previously simply did not honour his father.

41 This may well be another father issue, too. After all, Sarai was Abram's half-sister as well as his wife. Terah was her father so her problems with delay might stem from her judgements against him.

42 Yes, I know a lot of commentaries say this was a pre-incarnate Jesus. The angel theory has my vote for several reasons not least because this is a pre-eminent threshold covenant moment (and so angels are naturally there): the Israelites have just arrived in the Promised Land and have undertaken the rite of circumcision, the sign of the covenant with God.

43 Told to me personally by a Palestinian Christian whose father had lived in Jerusalem throughout World War I.

44 It's also interesting to note other political aspects in the wider story here. The city of Jerusalem— the capital of Judea and David's citadel—was in the territory of Benjamin. There's a double-edged sword in David's occupation of it and its subsequent rule by the kings of Judah. On the one side, Benjamin is a small tribe and the presence of Judah offers it protection. On the other, the kings of Judah obviously appropriated for themselves one of the finest fortresses in the region, because Benjamin couldn't really stop them taking it.

45 It's worth remarking on a couple of other incredible parallels in this epic story, one of which is to do with the name Jonathan, just to show how strong the pattern is. A man named Jonathan started the disaster; a case can be made for a Jonathan ending it. The priest of the hill country of Ephraim who had a concubine appears to have been named Jonathan. The text is pretty coy about identifying him, since apparently he was the grandson of Moses. (Some versions suggest Manasseh; however, this is to ignore the wordplay in the text. The 'n' of Manasseh—the only difference in Hebrew between that name and Moses—is a superscription in the text. Since Manasseh means *forget*, this wordplay is

there to indicate Jonathan had forgotten the legacy of Moses.) Not only was he responsible for starting a war that ended in genocide, he apparently went on to help the tribe of Dan set up a rival sanctuary which was eventually to include some golden calves! In yet another strong parallel, Jonathan, grandson of Moses, wasn't really entitled to be a high priest who wore an ephod: he was a Levite, rather than a descendent of Aaron. Just so, Samuel wasn't entitled to be a high priest, either. While he came from the hill country of Ephraim like Jonathan, and was a Levite (1 Chronicles 6:33–38), he was not descended from Aaron and thus not entitled to wear an ephod.

46 Also 'havatzelet' or 'chabatstseleth'.

47 http://www.abarim-publications.com/

48 See *God's Panoply: The Armour of God and the Kiss of Heaven*.

49 '*For God's gifts and His call are irrevocable.*' (Romans 11:29 AMP)

50 As well as other overtones. Within the poetry of the name (as opposed to the etymology) is 'tsaphah', *to look out or about, spy, keep watch, observe, watchman.*

51 Admittedly, from the description, it could be Python or Leviathan.

52 By 'worship without work', I mean worship that costs the worshipper nothing. Worship that looks more like entertainment than an offering to God.

53 There's an interesting thing here. After Uzzah's death, David was so discouraged he left the Ark at the house of Obed-Edom. God blessed Obed-Edom and finally David was encouraged to do the right thing in moving the Ark. Obed-Edom is appointed as a door-keeper—a guardian of the threshold. All of which is unremarkable except for the fact Obed-Edom is a Philistine.

Later in David's story, we encounter another foreigner guarding a threshold: Uriah the Hittite slept in the doorway when he returned from the war, rather than enter the house and enjoy the conjugal favour of his wife. Is there a subtle motif here: that a foreigner may safely guard a threshold where it's dangerous for the Israelites to do so? I am unsure whether this is indeed the case, but it is a recurring motif.

54 Some interesting circumstantial evidence supports the idea Leviathian was once a seraph, whose position was a minister of God's throneroom. The antechamber to the Holy of Holies in the tabernacle was a copy of that celestial throneroom and a place where the Levites ministered. In the antechamber was three items:

- a menorah
- an altar of incense
- table of showbread (*the bread of faces*)

The menorah or lampstand has seven 'heads', as Arthur Burk says Leviathan does. Certainly it has several since Psalm 74:17 specifies the 'heads of Leviathan'. It is the seraphim which are able to approach the heavenly incense altar, since in Isaiah 6:6 a seraph takes a coal from there to purify the prophet's lips. And the table of showbread, representing the feast in God's presence, may be paralleled in Jewish tradition which combines Job 40:30 with Isaiah 27:1 to conclude that Leviathan will be the first course at the great Messianic banquet.

55 My guess is that they are spirits which afflict us with silence, deafness and blindness. Their motto is like the three monkeys—*see no evil, hear no evil,*

speak no evil—except it might be better expressed as *don't see us as evil, don't hear our words as evil, don't speak of us as evil.* And whatever you do, don't recognise us as originating in pride.

56 Fourteen years later they were in a position to take possession of the land. The first seven years saw the battles for the land and the last seven saw the territorial division and appointing of boundaries for each tribe. Interesting to see in this instance that fourteen years is again associated with a threshold covenant. (See www.howardrollin.com/judeochristiangap/Gilgal.htm From this article, it would appear 14 years is the time for 'redemption of the land'—or 'healing', as we'd put it these days; after all, for the Jews, 'salvation' also meant 'healing'—and that it's about covenantal inheritance.) A time interval of fourteen is also associated with other threshold events: God explicitly gives instructions that fourteen days after the beginning of the month of Nisan, the Passover is to be kept. Also the Feast of Tabernacles (associated with the threshold event called the Transfiguration) is fourteen days into the month of Tishri.

57 Perhaps the gates of Eden should be counted.

58 Though spelt 'eb' in English in this particular instance.

59 *'Listen to Me, you who pursue righteousness, you who seek the Lord: look to the rock from which you were hewn, and to the quarry from which you were dug.'* (Isaiah 51:1 ESV)

60 Little wonder that Peter's letters are peppered with references to the church as living stones. Though some commentators suggest this emphasis on living stones may be an allusion to the trade which Jesus practised. Although widely regarded as a carpenter, He may have been a stone mason (or both carpenter and stone mason). *Tekton*, the word used to describe Him in the New Testament, is ambiguous. It could refer to working with wood or with stone.

61 The time it takes from the Feast of Booths to the Feast of Pentecost varies from year to year; however it is around 7½ to 8½ months.

62 On the way to the village of Emmaus after His resurrection, Jesus meets two of His disciples, one unnamed and the other called Cleopas. Of the dozens of post-resurrection appearances of Jesus, only a few were recorded in Scripture. Why Thomas? Why Mary Magdalene? Why Cleopas? Perhaps because each of them has a name which is so significant and symbolic, it became an inevitable and natural choice. Like Thomas and Mary Magdalene, I believe the story of Cleopas (basically the male version of Cleopatra) was chosen because he had a threshold-related name. *Glorious keys of the father.* How better to describe not only what Jesus had just been given from Heaven but what He passed on to Cleopas through His explanation of the Scriptures? It is probable that, as keys were representative of authority, Cleopas was the authority par excellence in the early church as to how Jesus' life and works fulfilled ancient prophecy. After all, it was Jesus Himself who'd told Cleopas just how it all lined up.

63 Ugarit was an ancient port city in Syria. The discovery of archives of Ugaritic literature in 1929 was of great significance to biblical scholarship, as these provided a detailed description of Canaanite religious beliefs from their own point of view.

64 The woman who had 'the issue of blood' (Mark 5:25–34) was said to come from here. She was allegedly so grateful to Jesus, she erected a votive statue in a gateway (c'mon! this is a threshold place, where else would it be?) to commemorate His gift of healing to her. Centuries later, it became famous during the time when Constantine relaxed the restrictions on Christianity—in part, because it came from the time of Jesus and was actually supposed to look like Him.

65 And of course if you know what a prophet is in Hebrew understanding—someone who discerns patterns and speaks them forth about them—you'll have laughed at that statement in *God's Poetry* about not being a prophet but only being able to discern what names mean. God really took me to task recently about rejecting His call and only describing what I had been given as a small corner of a prophet's mantle. It was foretelling that I feared; once it was made clear it is the forth-telling of pattern, I realised it wasn't something to be afraid of at all.

66 CE Arnold, *Power and Magic: The Concept of Power in Ephesians*, Wipf and Stock Publisher, Eugene Oregon, 2001.

67 Just how serious this problem is was brought home to me after I was at church at the beginning of the Advent season. The minister described his vestments as 'rose purple' to distinguish them from the 'violet purple' of Lent. I thought I'd investigate this when I got home. I typed "rose purple" in Google (with quotation marks to ensure I didn't get millions of hits on purple roses in the mix). I was interested to see when the first reference to Advent came up. It didn't. Not ever. I went right to the end, over 40 pages, refusing to give up. Finally I got to Google's helpful comment that there were some similar pages available, if I'd care to check those. But it was obvious they wouldn't help. Most pages were advertisements. However, when 'Advent' was added as a search term, I then got pages on colour symbolism in church vestments. 'Rose purple' represents the sky before dawn. This example only demonstrates I already needed to know the association before I could find it out. Google used to be a treasure trove where you could stumble across the most amazing facts—but not since the Information Age morphed into the Age of Advertisements.

68 'Stand firm' suggests one of the pillars in Solomon's Temple: Boaz, *strength*. In fact, it's possible these two verbal pillars are actually meant to suggest Boaz and Jachin, the great pillars of the First Temple. Boaz and Jachin are usually translated *strength* and *established*, but I've always felt there was more to it than was obvious. After long research I believe the names are allusive references to the morning and evening star. Erik Langkjer in *The Origin of Our Belief in God* (p. 276) connects Boaz to the morning star. His identification makes sense given the notorious difficulty of translating 'ayil', Hebrew for *strong leader*. In *God's Panoply* (p.37), I have noted 'ayil' can be translated *ram*, *oak*, *post* or *mighty man* and that its feminine form is actually part of the Hebrew name for the morning star. Langkjer suggests Bo'az is a cognate for 'Azizu, *strong one*, an Arabic name for the morning star.

Likewise Jachin, as the evening star, relies on a subtle parallel. Before Jachin was used as the name of a temple pillar, it was the name of one of the sons of Simeon. This son was also called Jarib (compare 1 Chronicles 4:24 with

Genesis 46:10), said to mean *God contends.* Jarib, however, rhymes with ''ereb', *evening*, from a root meaning *surety*. Thus *evening* has also got a similar subtly allusive feel to Jachin, *he will (securely) establish.*

69 *'The good Christian should beware the mathematician and all those who make empty prophecies. The danger already exists that the mathematicians have made a covenant with the devil to darken the spirit and to confine man in the bonds of hell.'* So said Augustine of Hippo. It's disconcerting actually, with thirty years of teaching mathematics under my belt, to find such a revered pillar of the early church combining mathematics and satanic covenants in the same thought. However Gnosticism and Pythagorean mathematical magic went hand in hand in those days (as they have whenever either one of them undergoes a resurgence) but the fact is that the work of the devil is always only a distorted copy. I find the incredible word-number fusions of the Hebrew and Christian Scriptures utterly inspiring. Which is why this book, as well as *God's Poetry* and *God's Panoply* ignores Augustine completely and crafts each section with its own mathematical design. The majority of the sections of this book are multiples of 111, like 555 or 777 or 888. Overall the length of the text is 51510 words (303×17×10) and these footnotes are 7777 words. 303 is chosen because it is the golden ratio of 490 which, at 70×7, represented the number of forgiveness throughout medieval literature. 17 is chosen because it is the number overwhelmingly favoured for design throughout the New Testament. It also shows up in many lists as, for example, how many things cannot separate us from the love of God. (See *Gawain and the Four Daughters of God: the testimony of mathematics in Cotton Nero A.x*, Anne Hamilton.)

70 Op. cit. p 19

71 Personally I think the protrusions are breasts. The city of Ephesus was, after all, said to have been founded by the Amazons: women who cut off their breasts to make it easier to use a bow and arrow. (Having done some archery in my time and having had the relevant part of my anatomy twanged between the string and the bow, with subsequent bruising for weeks, I can really understand the practicality of this move.)

72 CE Arnold, *Powers of Darkness: A thoughtful, Biblical look at an urgent challenge facing the Church*, Intervarsity Press, Leicester, 1992, p. 159. The second quote is from p 215 where model prayers are given for achieving such arming.

73 *'The wilderness and the solitary place shall be glad for them; and the desert shall rejoice, and blossom as the **rose**. It shall blossom abundantly, and rejoice even with joy and singing: the glory of Lebanon shall be given unto it, the excellency of Carmel and **Sharon**, they shall see the glory of the Lord, and the excellency of our God.'* (Isaiah 35:1–2 KJV)

74 *'I am the **rose** of **Sharon**, and the **lily** of the valleys.'* (Song of Solomon 2:1 KJV)

75 Acts 12:13–16.

76 The priests of the goddess Maat.

77 Missler points out that worship of Roma began in Smyrna in 196 BC; Caesar worship only began in the time of Augustus.

78 The best known Ephesia Grammata are a group of six words:

ΑΣΚΙ(ΟΝ) ΚΑΤΑΣΚΙ(ΟΝ) ΛΙΞ ΤΕΤΡΑΞ ΔΑΜΝΑΜΕΝΕΥΣ ΑΙΣΙΟΝ (or ΑΙΣΙΑ)
aski(on) kataski(on) lix tetrax damnameneus aision (aisia)
There were various attempts by ancient authors to make sense of the words. However, there is no certainty about the actual meaning or even that there is meant to be one.

79 The Roman soldier's shoes were made out of bronze or brass and consisted of tube-like greaves, connected by leather thonging to spiked soles. The greave was beautifully tooled metal beginning at the knee and extending down to the upper foot like a brass boot. The foot itself was covered with fine pieces of brass. www.sermoncentral.com/sermons/shoes-of-peace-dean-morgan-sermon-on-peace-86081.asp

80 They could have had As, Ans, Os—all Germanic in origin—or Deo, Dieu from Latin or French—or even something like Tiw, Tyr or Tue which is related to Deus and Zeus and has a connotation of honour.

81 Even though Yahweh doesn't mean this. Yahweh means 'he is who he is who he will be'. Heyeh is more correctly 'I am who I will be.'

82 2 Corinthians 11:4.

83 See *God's Poetry* (p. 117ff) for an examination of the seven titles which Jesus reclaimed from the principalities of other nations.

84 According to Plato, the Greek word for God, Theos, originates from the verb 'theein', meaning *to run*. St Gregory the Theologian identifies a second etymology beside the one of Plato: he claims Theos comes from the verb 'aithein', meaning *to be set alight, to burn, to be aflame*. St Basil the Great offers two more etymologies: 'God is called Theos either because He placed ('tetheikenai') all things, or because He beholds ('theasthai') all things.' http://orthodoxeurope.org/page/10/1.aspx

85 And, obviously, also words like *theme* and *antithesis*.

86 'In Ephesians 3:17, we find another mixed metaphor: "And I pray that you, being rooted and established in love..." The translators of the NIV have tidied up the mixed metaphor, which is more obvious in the original Greek, which reads more literally, "being rooted and founded in love." The first participle (*errizomenoi*) is an agricultural metaphor, based on the Greek word for 'root' (*riza*). The second participle is an architectural metaphor (*tethemeliomenoi*), based on the word for 'foundation' (*themelios*). Thus, in the mixed metaphor of Ephesians 3:17, we are to be connected to and based upon the love of Christ, as a tree is anchored through its roots and as a building rests upon its foundation.' ('Living in the Treehouse of God's Love', *The High Calling*, www.thehighcalling.org)

87 Klein writes that 'tris' as *shield* comes from the Greek 'thyreos', meaning *shield*, which in turn derives from the Greek 'thyra', *door*. (Going back to the Indo-European root, Klein shows that 'thyra' is cognate with the English word 'door' as well.) However, the connection between 'thyreos' and 'thyra' is strange: he writes that 'thyreos' is a *stone put against the door*: a shield. Thyroid also derives from 'thyreos'. The gland was given its name because of its similarity to ancient door-shaped shields.

88 In Luke 17:6, a very similar saying is reported but the 'mountain' is replaced by

a 'mulberry tree'.

89 This is a joke about Australia. New Zealand is made up of the North Island and South Island. When not referring to Australia as 'Aussie', Kiwis sometimes call it 'the West Island'.

90 Fans of *The Hitchhiker's Guide to the Galaxy* should realise here that the whale that falls from the sky is far from an original concept. It might seem like a product of the freakish imagination of Douglas Adams, but it has several precedents. In Norse mythology, the Vikings conceived of Bifröst as both a celestial fish and an aurora bridge spanning the gulf between heaven and earth.

Moreover in the original Grail legend—the initial one, where the mysterious word for 'grail' is used for the very first time—it is described as a green stone that falls from heaven, not as a cup or chalice. This grail is sometimes considered to have been moldavite: the impact melt from a meteorite strike in Germany that sent millions of glassy green tektites shooting so high that, as the earth spun beneath them, they landed in Czechoslovakia and beyond. The most valuable moldavite is called 'angel chimes' because it's said to sing when stroked against another piece.

91 Across many cultures the ash tree is a significant mythological symbol. In Norse, the World Ash Tree is central to words, worlds and weapons. Not a sword, however, but a spear.

92 Romans 1:9, 2 Corinthians 1:23.

93 A Reid, 'Exodus: Saved for Service', *Reading the Bible Today* series, Aquila Press, Sydney, 2013.

94 Strictly speaking, Truth in Hebrew is ''emeth', derived from ''aman'.

95 All of the gemstones of the breastplate of the High Priest are extremely hard to identify. Clues exist in the Septuagint, the Greek translation of the Hebrew Scriptures, but even on many of these scholars are divided. The name of one gem appears, however, to mean *dreamstone*. Because the most famous dreamer of the Old Testament was Joseph, it seems proper to assign it to either the tribe of Manasseh or Ephraim, since they were both his sons. In addition, the tribe of Ephraim had a sanctuary at Bethel, the very place where Jacob had a dream about a ladder reaching into heaven and angels ascending and descending it. So, it seems a good choice to pin amethyst as Ephraim's stone. Now, the Greeks considered the amethyst to be sacred to Dionysius, 'The True Vine', and as such, it was seen as a preventive for drunkenness. Ephraim is accused of drunken debauchery in Isaiah 28, so having a symbolic stone which allegedly prevented drunkenness and instead kept a drinker sober, alert and awake, seems to fit. This 'sober, alert, awake' aspect ties neatly to the spiritual connotations of the almond tree, its flowers and a watchman.

So, although there is no way to be sure amethyst is indeed the gemstone related to watchful prayers, this is my reasoning for believing it is likely to be so.

96 Another layer in Ephesians 6 may exist, referring to places Paul has visited. Yes, *another* layer above and beyond the Roman armour, kiss of heaven, mathematics of covenant, symbols of a threshold or cornerstone covenant, as well as the emblematic flowers and jewels signifying the truth behind the Ephesian Artemis

counterfeit! In this possible geographical layer there is, for instance, Caphtor, which as we have seen refers to both *helmet* and *pomegranate*. However, it also refers to the homeland of the Philistines which some suggest is Crete and others Cappadocia. Either way, Paul had been to both. Now the breastplate of righteousness is, as we have seen, an allusion to the rose of Sharon. But *rose* in Greek is the name of the island of Rhodes. Tick another place Paul has visited. In his allusive reference to *lilies* and *alabaster*, he could be directing attention to Susa, the ancient capital of the Persians. Perhaps in his years in Arabia, he made the trip there. There's also a possibility he refers to his hometown Tarsus. Although these few by no means make up a definite seventh layer of seven countries, the hint remains there is more here to be discovered. Like Jesus at Caesarea Philippi, subtly speaking healing to the land through His words to Peter, perhaps Paul is blessing the places he has visited in these written words.

97 The Hebrew word for *to kiss* is the same as for *to put on armour*. As I have demonstrated in *God's Panoply: The Armour of God and the Kiss of Heaven*, there is an allusion to a divine kiss in the finale to Paul's letter to the Ephesians where he famously discussed the Armour of God.

98 I'm not sure I agree with all I've read. I am particularly reluctant to take the advice of Win Worley in *Leviathan and Names of Other Spirits* to insist Leviathan manifest itself. This command alone may be legal grounds for retaliation. I cannot find any case where Jesus insisted a spirit manifest itself. Forcing it to do so may transgress the principle embodied in Jude 1:9. Apart from this, Worley's booklet is excellent—he points out Leviathan attempts to block our entrance to the Holy of Holies by robbing or deceiving us in the antechamber. Its many heads attempt to mimic the sevenfold lampstand, the smoke from its nostrils seeks to counterfeit the prayers of the incense altar with false religious experience and to cut us off from the showbread—the bread of the Presence of the Lord in His Word.

I remain convinced that honour is the key to dealing with Leviathan. Note the Israelites encountered killer snakes in the final year of their wilderness wanderings, right on the threshold of receiving their inheritance, when they grumbled. (Numbers 21) When we're disrespectful (even of God's provision), we may grant Leviathan or Python legal right to attack. Disrespect can take many forms. Consider the words of a God-fearing man on the verge of victory in a famous yacht race never ever lost by his home country: 'We cannot lose. God is an American.'

99 Such as 'Grace, grace to it!' (Zechariah 4:7) or 'The Lord knows who are His!' (2 Timothy 2:19) and many others.

100 For one woman, it took nearly 14 months. Admittedly there were seven seals to find. They were all odd; but they were all to do with tricking or being tricked.

101 Long-standing pre-existing covenants may also exist over your land. Such covenants may be name, salt, blood, threshold or any combination. In some instances, you may find yourself in a situation where your land or your inheritance is claimed by a principality. This makes it that much harder to contend for your own healing. Still, we should always remember: *if God is for us, who can be against us?*

Printed in Australia
AUOC02n0708041115
271453AU00002B/2/P

9 780980 362077